A Memoir

The Camp David Peace Accords:

35 years later: No War, No Peace

Sandy Simon

The Cedars Group
Delray Beach, Florida, 2013

Published by
The Cedars Group
220 MacFarlane Drive, Suite PH-6
Delray Beach, Florida 33483

Inquiries should be addressed to: sansimonjr@aol.com

© Sandy Simon, 2013

www.SandySimon.com

ISBN-13: 9781493630639

ISBN-10: 1493630636

What They're Saying

Mr. Simon has written an excellent well-researched book with great accuracy reflecting the events following the Egypt-Israeli peace agreement. I highly recommend this book to all Americans.

Andrew Killgore,
Former U.S. Ambassador to Qatar

I read this history lesson with joy and sadness. Joy because it was so clear and logical and sadness that the lessons you learned were either ignored or marginalized by our government. What was to come in the future should have been apparent to even the most junior Foreign Service officer. The peace that could have come and the lives that could have been spared had your wealth of knowledge and understanding of the regional sensitivities been incorporated into our foreign policy are too numerous to count. My hat is off to you for sharing these experiences.

Thomas A. Nassif, Former
U.S. Ambassador to Kingdom of Morocco

Mr. Simon's book accurately describes an important part of the history of the first steps by the organized Arab-American community to engage on this crucial matter. His story is an important period piece that should be of interest to Arab-Americans everywhere.

Nicholas Veliotes, Former
U.S. Ambassador to Jordan

Here is a fascinating, eye-witness, you-are—there account of an unusual mission—four Americans of Arab descent—travel to the Middle East in late 1978 to speak to the leaders of the Arab world and help facilitate an historic diplomatic breakthrough. Sandy Simon's account reads like a compelling novel, only the characters and events are very real! This story is an enlightening prelude to what turned into the Camp David Peace accords. An engrossing read!

**Peter Tanous, President of the American
Task Force for Lebanon and successful author**

As a member of our fact-finding delegation, I was well aware we were part of Arab American involvement in the political dialogue between the Arab world and the United States. Every American concerned about our role in the Middle East should read this book.

Sheryl Ameen, Art Historian

Other Books by Sandy Simon

The Immigrant

The Immigrant – Part 2

Sunrise Over Beirut

Beyond the Cedars

Remembering:
*A History of Florida's South Palm Beach County:
1894 to 1999*

The Amazing Story of Highland Beach,
Delray Beach and Boca Raton

A Stroke of Genius
*Messages of Hope and Healing From
a Thriving Stroke Survivor*

Camp David Accords

Beirut

Chapter ONE

Camp David Accords

Chapter 1
Beirut

We jumped when we heard the loud knock at the door.

It was midnight in Beirut.

Our four-person delegation was in Beirut in December, 1978 at the height of Lebanon's civil war that began in 1974.

We were quite a mix, all members of the National Association of Arab Americans (NAAA) executive committee: one Muslim, Dr. Hisham Sharabi, a brilliant and distinguished professor at Georgetown University and President of NAAA; Joe Baroody, incoming President of NAAA and a Melkite Christian; Sheryl Ameen, an Episcopalian of Druze heritage, Secretary of NAAA, an art historian focused on cross-cultural and historic art; and me, Senior Vice President of NAAA, an Episcopalian of Greek Orthodox heritage. We were a microcosm of Lebanon's society. We all felt a strange mix of emotions: excitement, determination, fascination, privilege, and a natural sense of apprehension about taking on this important fact-finding mission.

The Arab world had severed all diplomatic ties with the United States and Egypt when, under President Carter's guidance, the Camp David Accords between Egypt and Israel were signed that September 17, 1978.

The Arab world was livid, angry at Anwar Sadat and President

3

Carter for not assuring a regional peace. In essence, they were ratifying Israel's taking of Arab lands during their surprise attacks in June, 1967 during the Six-Day War.

None of us had any idea what we were going to face, but we were all anxious to do what we could to fulfill our mission of intercommunication and determination of the positions of the leadership of key Arab nations *vis-à-vis* the agreement between Egypt and Israel.

That night, after fourteen days of meetings with eight heads of state, we were waiting for word from the Palestinian Liberation Organization (PLO) about our final meeting, a possible meeting with Chairman Yassir Arafat, a former civil engineer in Kuwait, who for several years had been leader of the principal opposition to Israel's taking of Palestine, and branded a terrorist by Israel and the United States.

We had learned so much from this trip, but now, finally, we were to meet with the one man so hated in Israel and much of the United States who both viewed him as a terrorist responsible for hundreds of bombings and deaths.

Chapter 2
The Phone Call

In November, 1978, a representative of the State Department contacted the NAAA in Washington, D.C. seeking its assistance. The NAAA was well known as the principal advocate for closer relations between the Arab world and the U.S., a counter advocate to the American Israeli Public Affairs Committee (AIPAC), Israel's principal political advocate in the U.S.

At the time, I was serving my fourth year as Senior Vice President of NAAA, which was comprised mostly of first generation Syrian and Lebanese Americans, with a growing membership of Palestinian Americans. Dr. Hisham Sharabi spoke fluent Arabic and was a Palestinian by birth. Joe Baroody's father, William Baroody, also of Lebanese heritage, founded the American Enterprise Institute in Washington.

Within two days after that contact, like the other three, I received a phone call at my home in Atlanta from David Sadd, Executive Director of the NAAA. His first words were, "Sandy, would you be willing to go to the Middle East on a fact-finding mission at the request of Secretary of State Cyrus Vance and President Carter?"

I was pleasantly stunned by his question and because for more than five years I had been deeply engrossed in the study of Middle East issues, wanted to travel to the region of my ancestors, Lebanon and Syria, and was active in efforts to encourage peace in that region, I immediately answered, "Of course I will, David!"

All Americans, including me, were very much aware of the recent Camp David Accords negotiations hosted by President Carter that purportedly brought peace between Israel and Egypt, and, hopefully, to the entire Middle East. But those of us in the NAAA knew the importance of the creation of a Palestinian state, Israel's return of lands captured by Israel during the Six-Day War in 1967, just eleven years earlier, and the lack of their inclusion in the Accords. We were convinced Israel's Begin would likely never agree to these terms, in contradiction of U.N Resolutions 242 and 338, which Israel had supported earlier. We also believed the Arabs would accept nothing less. But now we were being asked to meet with the heads of Arab governments and high officials to find out what they were thinking, what they wanted, and what were their true nonpublic views of the Israel-Egypt Peace Treaty documented in the Camp David Accords.

Now, to the fourteen-day "blizzard" mission!

Chapter 3
The Mission

About a week later, David Sadd called again to say all arrangements had been made through the State Department, and gave the scheduled meeting date at JFK for our flight to Amman, Jordan via Jordan's Alia Airlines.

On the morning of December 7, 1978, Sheryl and I agreed to meet at the New York City residence of Ambassador Ghassan and Mrs. Tueni, the Lebanese ambassador to the United Nations (UN).

Following a delightful lunch and discussion of our impending trip to begin later that evening, I took Sheryl to Wall Street where a good friend of mine worked on the floor of the New York Stock Exchange (NYSE). It was exciting for both of us to experience the hectic pace of traders making contracts with pads and pens, displaying the very essence of free enterprise and capitalism of the U.S. While we were there, the market got quite volatile as a result of an untrue rumor that President Anwar Sadat had been assassinated. It was a shock to us, of course, because we were leaving that night for the Middle East and that news, if true, could have created unknown chaos throughout the Middle East just as we were arriving. We were very happy to learn later that it was simply a rumor.

Later in the afternoon, we taxied to JFK to begin what would become the most extraordinary trip of our lifetimes, guests of the State

Department, interactions with heads of state and high officials in eight angry Arab countries with whom the U.S. had no communications.

We were filled with anticipation and excitement as the four of us finally arrived at the departure gate. Just boarding the Boeing 747, being ushered by the gracious Jordanian stewardesses to the very front of the first class section was exhilarating. As I took my seat, I found myself sitting next to Mr. Najeeb Halaby, who became famous when his daughter, Lisa, married King Hussein of Jordan and became Queen Noor. At that time, his background became significantly noted in the U.S. media. I recalled reading about him and was fascinated by this prominent, iconic man born in Dallas, Texas, with the same heritage as mine: first generation Christian Syrian-Americans. His father, Elias Halaby, emigrated to the U.S. in 1891. My mother and her parents, Syrian Christians too, arrived in America in 1905. My paternal grandfather, a Christian Lebanese, arrived in Delray Beach, Florida, in 1912. My father, having to wait until World War I ended, joined his father in 1920.

Mr. Halaby was the second Administrator of the U.S. Federal Aviation Administration (FAA) from 1961-1965, Chairman and CEO of Pan American Airlines from 1969-1972 and was present at the christening of the first Boeing 747, the same plane we were now flying to Amman. He was a proponent for the creation of a new Department of Transportation, which came into being while he was part of Lyndon Johnson's administration.

Mr. Halaby, I found, had an amazing personal history and a wonderful sense of humor. His maternal grandfather served in the 7th Tennessee Cavalry in the Civil War. After attending boarding school in Michigan, he graduated from Stanford University and Yale Law School.

He was a U.S. Navy test pilot during World War II and on May 1, 1945, made history by making the first solo transcontinental jet flight from California to Maryland in just five hours and forty minutes. After the war, he was the U.S. State Department's civil aviation advisor to King Ibn Saud of Saudi Arabia and helped establish Saudi Arabian Airlines.

We carried on a lively conversation getting to know each other. He was very positive about our mission, advising me on his perspective. We even shared some humorous stories. We laughed together as I shared some of my favorite jokes. I experienced a rush of elation and adrenalin simply sitting next to Mr. Halaby, a renowned American, quite famous in his own right.

After the plane reached cruising altitude, Mr. Halaby left his seat and went to the small closet ahead of us at the bulkhead, removed his coat and hung it up. (Only he would and could have known to do that.) We were all impressed when he also removed two blankets and two pillows, spread them on the floor near the bulkhead, lay down and went fast sleep in great comfort. I winked at Sheryl across the aisle and asked for the teddy bear a child nearby had dropped on the floor.

I boldly reached for the stuffed teddy bear, stepped to the prone Najeeb Halaby, and with a smile, placed the teddy bear at his cheek and shoulder, and took two photographs of him. Much later, he awoke, looked directly at the teddy bear, then at me, and laughed so hard I thought he was going to choke. I laughed too as I told him, "Not to worry, I'm giving you the photographs!"

"Photographs?"

"Yes," I replied. "I thought at first I'd hand them to King Hussein so he'd know the truth about his father-in-law."

We enjoyed a martini together and kept laughing, imagining the expression on King Hussein's face as he heard the stories and looked over the photos.

Alia Airlines flight: NYC to Amman, Jordan;
Najeeb Halaby and Sheryl Ameen with Joe Baroody.

Hasham Sharabi, Sandy Simon and Joe Baroody

Camp David Accords

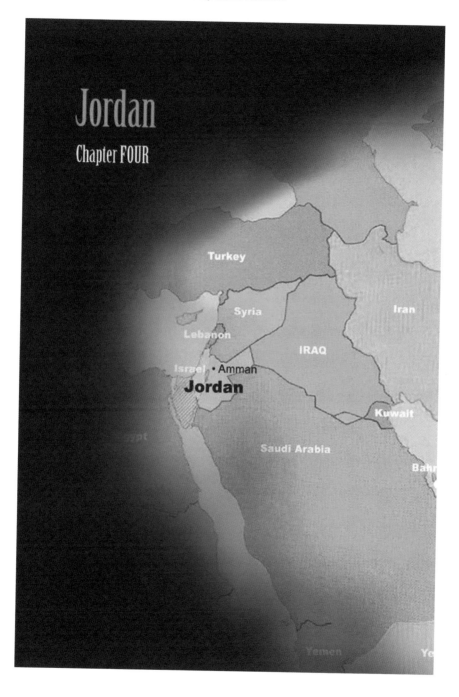

Jordan
Chapter FOUR

Camp David Accords

14

Chapter 4
Jordan

Amman, Jordan was the first stop for us. Thankfully for us, Dr. Sharabi accomplished extraordinary scheduling of all our appointments with the highest officials of all the nations we visited. Our first visit was with U.S. Ambassador Nicholas Veliotes at his offices across the street from our hotel, The Intercontinental. He was most impressive with his knowledgeable analysis of the tense situation, and perhaps the only U.S. ambassador who had any sort of communication with the government he was to deal with. He seemed sympathetic to the king's plight because so many penniless Palestinian refugees had entered Jordan during the 1947 war, and became a major proportion of Jordan's population. During and after the 1967 war, an additional hundreds of thousands, maybe millions, of Palestinians had fled into Jordan.

In anticipation of Ambassador Veliotes' comments, I pulled out my yellow legal pad and asked if he'd mind if I took notes. He nodded his assent and began:

"Thousands of refugees, especially those who were successful in Palestine, have opened offices and shops here in Jordan, whether they are businessmen, doctors, dentists, engineers, attorneys or shop keepers. Amman, of course, has received most of those refugees, plus thousands of the poor and homeless, putting a strain on the city and the nation's economy, to say nothing of the political turmoil. Nearly all the refugees arrived with only their belongings on their backs and what they carried. And most continue to yearn deeply to return to their

15

homes and property in Palestine."

Ambassador Veliotes continued, "King Hussein is under intense pressure, and at a crossroads. The king desperately wants peace in the region and would support Egypt's peace treaty in the context of a regional peace settlement, including all lands taken by Israel in 1967, namely East Jerusalem, the West Bank, Gaza, and Syria's Golan.

"I don't believe any Arab state, aside from Egypt, will sign a peace treaty with Israel unless there is a provision for a Palestinian state. If Egypt does so, they will be isolated in the Arab and Muslim worlds."

Hisham asked the ambassador, "Are you saying if Egypt signs this treaty with Israel without a Palestinian state, they will be alone?"

"That is exactly what I am saying." Then, he added, "I understand you have an appointment with King Hussein. Is that correct?"

"Yes, we do, Mr. Ambassador, this afternoon, in two hours at his residence."

"Understand, King Hussein feels deeply offended by Sadat's individual initiative. Jordan, after all, has the most to lose with an Egyptian-Israel treaty. He feels humiliated and is very angry with Sadat. King Hussein feels betrayed even by the United States, having met with President Carter and Secretary Vance very recently when they discussed joint efforts toward a regional peace treaty.

"Let me help you, America is not very popular in the region, and we have to be very careful. Not with the government, but so many angry citizens, including very outraged Palestinian refugees. So, I am going to loan you my car. It's well-reinforced with bulletproof doors and windows, one inch steel underneath, and I'll have my bodyguards drive you for your protection.

"Please note," the ambassador added, "the governments and the people of the countries you are visiting are very upset with the Unites States. They don't understand America not acting in its own best interests in the Middle East. For decades, the Arab nations have admired and supported the United States. Saudi Arabia and the Gulf states have been delivering huge amounts of its oil at very low prices to America and the West since the early 1930s, and assured President Roosevelt of a guaranteed supply during World War II. The price paid to the Arab oil exporting nations for nearly forty years was nearly the same price, about $2.50 to $3.00 per barrel all those years, while prices of goods they purchased from the West, including automobiles, trucks, steel, aluminum, equipment and other products increased ten times during the same period. The Arabs believe they continue to be America's best friends and don't understand why or agree that America doesn't require Israel to return the lands they took in 1967.

"I expect you'll hear this position everywhere you go. You know that the Palestinians have been the technocrats operating most utilities and institutions in each of the countries you are visiting, and not only are they well-educated and highly respected, but are true blood cousins, members of extended families as is the culture here in the Arab world.

"Of course," he added, "as King Hussein knows, too many Arab countries are ruled by despots and dictators. They themselves are guilty of depriving their citizens of freedom and true human rights. They govern their press, eliminate opposition, and deprive their young

17

people from excellent education, jobs, and hopeful futures.

"Even the Palestinians don't help their cause with attacks on Israeli citizens, using kidnapping, car bombs, and young people as guerilla fighters. Israel, while not innocent, certainly does a better job for their people in education, progress in agriculture, and technological advancements which outshines those of us in the Arab world. As Muslims, they pray all day, do not understand that they are in a global technological awakening, that they are not keeping up with the rest of the world, especially the United States, and even Israel," the ambassador concluded.

Our entirely constructive and informative meeting ended after two intense informative and very gratifying hours. As we all rose to leave for our meeting with the king, he said to us, "I would appreciate another meeting with you after your meeting with King Hussein."

After we left the embassy, we prepared to meet the King that at least three of us respected so highly. We agreed we learned a lot from the ambassador, not only of Jordan's situation, but of all the nations we were about to visit.

"Sandy," Sheryl said to me as we left the ambassador's offices, "I am really inspired by Ambassador Veliotes' insight and apparent intimacy with King Hussein."

"I agree, Sheryl. He obviously not only well represents the interests of the United States, but is very much aware of what is happening in Jordan, especially with the major problems facing the King as a result of the enormous influx of hundreds of thousands of Palestinian refugees culturally, politically and economically.

"He was clear about the anger of so many in Jordan feeling heightened anger toward the Israel-United States alliance."

"What do you think about the ambassador's comments, Sandy?" Sheryl asked me as we sat in the back of the ambassador's large bullet-proof chase car.

"Exhilarated," I replied, "I really like Ambassador Veliotes. He's so intelligent, forthcoming, and told us a lot I didn't and most Americans don't know. I think no one realizes the devastating impact on so many people, mothers, children, struggling farmers being brutally removed from their homes and their livelihood. They have had their lives torn apart by being forced from their homes, and how great the burden was for neighboring countries like Jordan, Lebanon and Syria.

"We all know about the horrible treatment Jews had to bear in Europe over the centuries, the Russian Pogroms when they were removed from their homes, farms and villages. How painful that must have been.

"And, how about the Spanish and French Inquisitions where so many were killed, imprisoned, tortured and exiled simply because they were Jews.

"Jews worldwide believe Israel is their 'safe haven' from persecution. The right-wing extremist Likud leaders claimed before the Six Day War they were too vulnerable and not secure.

"There is an enormous difference between being of the Jewish faith and being a hardline Zionist. "Since the late 1800s, Zionists in Europe have had the goal of taking all of Palestine, cleansing it of all non-Jews by removing them by force. Jews believe in the Law of

19

Moses, especially of the Ten Commandments. The Torah has been used and abused by the Zionists."

"For sure, Israel was just about nine miles wide in some places, so they claim they felt insecure."

(L-R) Sandy Simon, Joe Baroody, Sheryl Ameen, U.S. Ambassador Nicholas Veliotes, and Hisham Sharabi

**King Hussein of Jordan with (L-R) Joe Baroody,
Hisham Sharabi and Sandy Simon**

**King Hussein of Jordan, U.S. Ambassador to Saudi Arabia
John C. West, and Sandy Simon**

21

Hisham leaned back and said, "As a Palestinian, I can say that the Palestinian people feel badly about what Jews in the diaspora have been subjected to, especially what the Germans and the French did to them in what they call 'The Holocaust.' But," he added, "they are doing the same thing to the Palestinian people, and the United States supports their ethnic cleansing.

"The Zionist goal is to create a purely Jewish state with absolute, guaranteed security.   But, there is no such thing as guaranteed security for any state. And besides, they keep increasing their borders. That, in a nutshell is what the Arab world is facing."

* * * * *

As we drove from the city we noted it was late in the afternoon. As we were driven westward toward King Hussein's residence, we saw all around us on the rolling hills, thousands of acres of young forests of pine trees, olive groves and even young date palms recently planted by joint ventures of public and private joint ventures, just as the ambassador told us."

"In a way, Jordan is indeed 'greening the desert,'" Sheryl replied.

As we neared the king's residence, we saw his white one story home on a   hill, surrounded by immaculate areas of trees, grass and well cared for grounds. His residence itself was a beautiful, quite impressive white edifice of stone facing with large double entry doors.

22

We knew that the king, understood to be a direct descendant of Mohammed, was highly revered by his citizens for his fair-handed government and his growing acceptance of citizen involvement in the Parliament. We anxiously followed our driver and escort to the entry where we were warmly welcomed by the king himself! He graciously welcomed us by customarily embracing each of us and exchanging kisses on our cheeks.

"What a wonderful, warm welcome!" Sheryl whispered to me as we followed him into his large, spacious living room elegantly furnished with silk damask covered couches and arm chairs. The entire floor of marble tiles was covered with magnificent oriental carpets.

He directed us to the cluster of couches and chairs nearest the wall of glass windows through which we could easily see buildings in Jerusalem.

After cordially inviting us into his living room, and offering tea, King Hussein patiently and graciously shared his knowledge only he had including his surreptitious meetings with high officials of Israel hoping to find some sort of resolution toward peace in the region. But he conveyed his deep disappointment and frustrations with the Israeli Likud government and the total financial and military support given them by America that supports their recalcitrance.

"Many in the Arab World believe the overwhelming military power of Israel to be destructive of the stability, prosperity and happiness of the entire Middle East, if not the world.

"We would like to see their military power reduced to a level so that Israel can defend itself and fulfill its moral duties. We also believe somehow, some way, a regional peace in the region can indeed happen. But it may have to wait for the current Likud leadership to be replaced by their Labor Party."

I repeated the same request to the king to take notes as I had with the ambassador.

"Our people simply don't understand America's continued financial and military support enabling them to take others' lands, build settlements on them and claim the lands of Palestine as their own." He sighed. "Palestine was a happy place and Palestinians were a happy people — very well educated, very spiritual, talented and friendly. But they have been harshly abused by the massive influx of Zionists. And this treaty between Israel and Egypt, without provisions of a Palestinian state and recompense, will be a failure with dire consequences in the coming years. No other Arab country can possibly join in without those provisions. Certainly not Jordan. We are a country without wealth, mostly arid desert, no oil, no major army or air force. We cannot war with Israel, which is so heavily armed by the United States."

King Hussein seemed agonized by the conditions and continued influx of millions of Palestinian refugees that his very much "Confrontation State" with Israel suffered as a result of the harsh and rigidly unforgiving treatment of the Palestinian people. This was especially exacerbated by Begin's Likud Party and the U.S. position of heavily favoring support of Israel's illegal actions. I am very concerned that the Palestinians are desperate and the young men feel they have no future, no reason for hope. And as you know, desperate people do desperate things when they lose hope.

"We do believe President Carter is a good man, that he cares deeply for the principles of America, of human rights for everyone, justice and democracy, even for the Palestinians. We are also aware that the pro-Israel support in the U.S. is overwhelmingly successful in Washington in your Senate and Congress.

"What we, throughout the Arab world and the Muslim world, fear is that the U.S. support of Israel's treatment of the Palestinians is so unjust that Israel and the U.S. are becoming hated by some angry young men who see no future for themselves. The issue has become fodder for recruiting young Muslim men to become extremists, with many ripe for recruitment into the extremist and Islamist movement. We oppose the bombings, rockets, and attacks by the PLO on Israel, but they deeply resent their families' lands and homes being taken by the Zionists. If this continues over the next ten to twenty years, I fear secular pro-West governments in the Arab world will be seriously threatened, perhaps overthrown by the Islamist movement. It could also cause these angry, frustrated, educated young men to be recruited to attack U.S. interests throughout the world. It is urgent that the U.S. make Israel accept a Palestinian state, vacate all lands taken in 1967 in Syria, Jerusalem, the West Bank, and Gaza. Only then will Israel have peace, recognition, and the security it claims is their goal. The future does not look favorable for pro-Western Arab governments nor for the United States if a regional peace does not happen. The genie is almost out of the bottle. It will be near to impossible for it to be put back in the bottle once out. And if the Islamists, like in Iran, overthrow Saddam Hussein in Iraq or Hafez Al Assad in Syria, it is very possible they could become rigidly Islamist, threatening Jordan, Lebanon, and Israel.

"Please convey these beliefs to your good President who seems alone in seeking human rights in Palestine despite the U.S. political forces that ignorantly support Israel as they do. The path the U.S. and Israel are on is not in their long-term best interests! The Arabs do not hate Jews. They are our Biblical cousins. But we do resent the right wing

Zionists' actions against our people."

As Sheryl had prepared well, she had her Nikon camera and I had mine. So we asked the king if he would honor us by allowing photographs with him.

He smiled and replied, "Of course, it would be my privilege."

During our second meeting with Ambassador Veliotes, we shared what we had learned from King Hussein. He listened intently with understanding and gratitude, nodding often a he listened to each of us give our separate perspectives of our meeting with King Hussein, much of which he had not heard directly from the King. We discussed with him the King's concern with the heavy economic and political burden on Jordan and the King's concern about the sense of desperation and growing anger among the young Palestinian refugees toward Israel and the United States, and what that could become if they became convinced that they had nothing more to lose. We asked him what he believed the U.S. needs to do to bring other Arab leaders to the table and negotiate with the Israelis. The ambassador believed the President was accomplishing more than any other U.S. president had to bring peace to the region. He considered Anwar Sadat's efforts as a good and positive move, but said that until the Israelis elect a more moderate government that will vacate the West Bank, the Golan, Gaza and East Jerusalem as Israel had agreed to do under U.N. resolutions, there could be no regional peace.

We hoped during our upcoming visits with other heads of state that some ideas would emerge that would somehow lead to a breakthrough in the politics of the region.

* * * * *

In the early evening, after our incredible first two appointments, we gathered on the outdoor terrace of The Intercontinental Hotel for cocktails and local delicious Jordanian almonds and a group recap of the day's events. The weather was perfect: clear skies, gentle light cool breezes, dry air. We were ecstatic while ruminating over our first wonderful meetings, and listened to the calls for prayers emanating from several minarets, mainly the singing of imams broadcast across the city.

Besides taking notes on the yellow legal pads, so that I'd have a record of everything said as much as possible and, since Sheryl and I brought cameras, we were fortunate to end up with a number of photographs to remember the visits. We discussed our individual perspectives on the meetings that day. Luckily, Sheryl took excellent notes as well.

Dr. Sharabi commented, reflecting his Palestinian and social views, "I have never liked the idea of royalty in our region, and I don't like kingdoms. But," he continued, "I was very impressed with King Hussein. Very impressed."

"Hisham," I asked after we returned to the hotel, "King Hussein obviously seeks a regional peace and cares deeply about the Palestinian refugees. But if the PLO and others continue to attack Israeli citizens, all they are accomplishing is a hardening of the anger of the Israelis. Wouldn't you agree that stopping those attacks would calm the situation?"

"My friend, you are being naïve, and by living in safety in America, you cannot feel the frustration and growing anger of our young people. They have no American jets, rockets, tanks and an army so to attempt with force against the Israelis to get back their homeland, their homes, groves, their land. No one seems to care in the West. Our human rights, given by Allah, God, have been taken by the Israeli belief that 'might makes right.' This is not justice, and I am not sure anyone can stop these young men who have lost all hope and faith in God."

"But, Hisham, what is the difference between a Jewish mother and child being blown up by a bomb or an Arab mother and child being blown to death or maimed by a bomb? It's got to stop somewhere. The Jewish people have suffered so much over the centuries to the point where they feel they can only be safe in their own country."

"I understand what you are saying, Sandy, but the Arabs did not cause suffering of the Jewish people. Why then must we be robbed of our human rights because of what the Europeans did to them?"

"Hisham," I replied, "both sides must stop the violence, both sides are to blame, both sides. To me," I quickly continued, "the past is history. It is the present and the future we must focus on. And I believe both sides must stop the violence, both sides."

Joe interjected as we sat at the table on the hotel's terrace, "Only America's political leadership can bring about peace in the region, and clearly, the current U.S. government intends to enable Israel to be impenetrable."

"Excuse me," a well-dressed man spoke to us as he arrived at

28

our table, "I could not help overhearing some of your conversation. You are Americans?"

Joe looked up at the man and spoke first, "Yes we are. Can we help you?"

"Well, I am a Palestinian businessman now living in Amman. Can you help me understand why the United States is so captured by the Israeli lobby and arms the Israelis so much? I mean, for a tiny country to be the third most militarily powerful nation in the world is an extraordinary situation, don't you think? I mean, why do the Americans hate the Arabs so much and stand by Israel no matter how much they abuse the Palestinian people?"

Joe replied, "Most Americans are Christian, and a large, active part of them are convinced that the state of Israel is God's will. Christians in America from our founding hundreds of years ago believed themselves to be of Judaic Christian belief."

"But," the businessman said, "there is another aspect to this. The pro-Israel lobby is so effective and successful at selling their case to the American public and to the U.S. Senators and Congressmen. One has to admire how diligently they work and contribute hundreds of millions of dollars to campaigns of the Congressmen and Senators. Perhaps we should emulate their model of financial contributions to political campaigns.

"I don't think the Arabs or Arab Americans understand the political world and how it works. Most Arab Americans simply go about their enterprises, caring for their families and supporting their churches. They don't feel visceral danger to their lives or their culture, so, fellow Arab Americans are not afraid like the pro-Israel Jews. And, in the view of the Arabs their cause is just; that lobbying politicians is not, in their view, necessary because God will bring justice."

"So," I commented, "how do we change that view here and in America? Not only that, but the fact is, Christians are taught Bible stories, mostly from the Old Testament, from childhood, including Adam and Eve, the Garden of Eden, Abraham, God's saving Isaac, Noah's Ark, Jonah and the whale, Daniel's lion's den and that the early Hebrews were "chosen" by God as descendants of Abraham, Isaac and that God brought them out of slavery in Egypt."

"But," the gentleman interjected, "they wrote the Old Testament, didn't they? I mean it suits their purpose, doesn't it? We believe the Hebrews were chosen by God to teach the world of the living, loving God to be a 'Light Unto The World,' not 'chosen' to take what they want and do what they wish! We Muslims and Arabs are convinced that Ishmael was Abraham's eldest son of him and Hagar, and thus was the son God saved, not Isaac who was the younger brother and as a result, Ishmael is the first descendant of Abraham and because Hagar was Egyptian, Arabs believe they are the true descendants of Abraham, you see? We and the Jews are cousins. We do not hate the Jewish people. In many ways we admire them. Many are intelligent, enterprising, generous, philanthropic, talented, and they have revered their religious heritage better than any group over the centuries. We Arabs hate what the Germans did to them. But we also are adamantly opposed to the Zionist goals of recreating the Israel of King David, which means all of Palestine, part of the Golan, and parts of Lebanon and, Syria. Some say they want to control all lands from the Nile to the Euphrates River, in Iraq. We who have lived in these lands since before Moses and Joshua arrived must resist their taking of all of Palestine. We would be happy with our own state, freedom in just the

30

West Bank, only 20 percent of what was Palestine before the Zionist onslaught, you see?

"And Israeli propaganda is so convincing of the Americans. They say the Arabs want to kill all Jews, or that the Arabs want to drive them into the sea. That is so ridiculous. They say we teach our children to hate Jews. That is not true. What the Israelis do to our children and to their parents in front of their children causes hatred. In God's name we do not want to do those terrible things. And we couldn't anyway. We have stones to throw. Israel has the most overpowering military machine, America's most advanced technology, training and, sadly, their political leaders are so militant! You see?

"Mr. Begin thinks he is a modern day Joshua, killing everyone in his way and taking others' land. He is behaving like King Ahab, as you see in the book of Kings. No, we do not believe this state of Israel is God's will. We believe God is love and forgiveness, and does not condone war and killing. There is a local joke. It goes like this: 'What is the difference between God and Menachem Begin? The answer is: God does not think he is Menachem Begin'."

We smiled at his joke, thinking, maybe that is not a joke.

"In addition," I added, "our media and politicians have reminded the American people a sense of empathy, throughout America that America is not blameless for the horrors put on the Jewish people by the Nazis and that America did nothing to absorb them or stop Hitler when he was killing so many Jews. There is a sense of guilt and great empathy for the Jewish people."

"I can understand that, because America refused to accept Jewish Europeans after World War II, but pressed the British to permit hundreds of thousands of them to come here and take our lands. Why?"

I think we all felt we had done all we could, including two meetings with Ambassador Veliotes, a lengthy but extraordinarily informative three hour visit with King Hussein, and a lengthy conversation with the visitor to our table when we got an earful of the Palestinian perspective.

We were tired and looking forward to our flight to Kuwait. Soon after the gentleman's visit we returned to our rooms for the night.

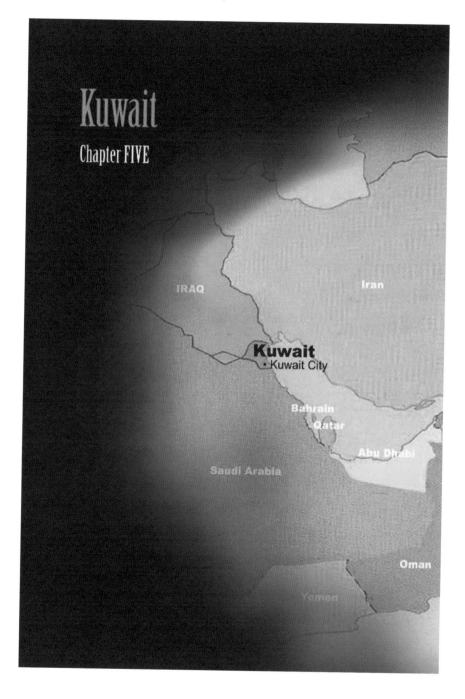

Kuwait
Chapter FIVE

Camp David Accords

Chapter 5
Kuwait

The next morning we met with Ali Ghandour, chairman of Alia Airlines. Mr. Ghandour, a brilliant, charming, positive executive, applauded our mission and shared his insight and advice, which was "right on." Apparently, with King Hussein's approval, he kindly offered us an Alia Airlines Lear jet and pilots at our disposal so that we could actually accomplish our tasks of visiting seven more countries in such a short time.

We flew to Kuwait City where, at around ten o'clock p.m., we checked into our hotel across the fully landscaped six-lane divided boulevard from the Persian Arabian Gulf. We could see the U.S. Embassy and its turquoise swimming pool from our windows, just a block away to the north, and the Gulf beaches just across the boulevard. The city was quite modern, with contemporary designs of its buildings and other structures.

I was pretty excited to be here in Kuwait. After we checked into our hotel next to the U.S. embassy, I suggested we all walk over to the beach and walk in the shallows of the Persian Gulf. The air was cool and dry as it caressed our faces with a light breeze off the Gulf.

"We may not get another chance to walk in the waters of the Persian Gulf," I said to Sheryl and Joe as we crossed the divided six-lane boulevard to the beach.

The sands were firm and the water was quite calm and cool,

even peaceful. Calm and peaceful were contrary metaphors, we agreed, that were in contradiction to the angry politics of the region, but in a way, described the differences between the tensions along the eastern Mediterranean Sea and the Gulf States.

While Sheryl and Joe looked around searching for shells, I rolled up my pant legs and walked in the calm waters.

"I just had to, Sheryl. The Persian Gulf was urging me to step in," I said, laughing.

Sandy Simon with Ali Ghandour, Chairman, Alia
Airlines, Joe Baroody, Sheryl Ameen

* * * * *

Our first meeting the next morning was with Sheikh Ali Al Sabah, a popular member of the royal family, who had just returned from Washington where he was Kuwait's Ambassador and a close friend of all of us. Now he was serving as Kuwait's Minister of Defense.

"*Ahlen!* Welcome, my dear friends!" Sheikh Ali's familiar jovial smile and outstretched arms contrasted significantly with our earlier formal meeting with King Hussein in Amman. To be sure, the mood of the people in the Gulf contrasted sharply with the people in what they call "Confrontation States," i.e., those states bordering or nearby Israel: Egypt, Jordan, Syria, Lebanon, and Iraq. Even though Iraq had no common border with Israel, Iraq too qualified for that designation.

Kuwait and the other Gulf States, next on our itinerary, were clearly distant politically and geographically to those states. But, being Arab and Muslim, they strongly supported their brothers and sisters of the "Confrontation States."

Right away, Sheikh Ali's assistant, following Arab custom, entered with a tray of hot tea, orange juice, and soda. We sat and visited, conversing intensely, for several hours, seeking Sheikh Ali's insight regarding Kuwait's relationship with America. We all knew him well during his years in Washington.

"We, the people of Kuwait, love America!" he exclaimed, flashing his wide smile and sparkling white teeth contrasting with his olive skin, and black mustache and goatee. He was, of course, wearing his white *dishdash* (loose fitting gown) and kiffeyeh (headdress), typical of the Gulf States, including his *ghutra* (black and white checkered scarf) atop his head, held in place with his *aghal* (a black circled rope). He could not have been more congenial.

"How do you like being the new Minister of Defense as compared to being Ambassador to the United States?"

He laughed aloud as he said, "In Washington, my wife and I attended hundreds of receptions, we hosted many receptions as you know because you all came to be with us, and we are grateful for our friendship. Here, it is different for me.

"Ever since the price of oil increased so much five years ago from $3.50 per barrel to $19 per barrel, Kuwait, like the Emirates and Saudi Arabia are awash in billions of dollars we never had before. We have been undergoing a complete transformation," he continued as he gesticulated with his hands, "from mud houses and a fourteenth century economy and culture, to Western-style homes. Six years ago only the wealthiest had television, now everyone has a dish on their homes and they buy films from America and Europe. It is an amazing time for us.

"We are building boulevards, new water treatment plants, desalinization facilities, water and waste treatment plants, office buildings, schools, and hospitals. We have a new museum also that you must visit while you are here."

"Do you have many American firms doing work for you?"

"Oh, yes. The Americans are the best. Parsons and Bechtel did most of our early planning and construction. They are good, aren't they? They have completely redesigned Kuwait City, planned our residential and commercial boulevards, subdivisions, utilities, and electrical power system. We operate with natural gas that used to be burned and wasted at the wells. And our oil exports have increased even with the so-called OPEC embargo you hear so much about on your television. There really is no shortage of oil. It is truly the oil companies and Wall Street who are causing the gasoline shortages, not us."

"How do you select what projects and companies you enlist?"

He laughed aloud again and, rising from his damask-covered chair, beckoned for us to join him as he led us to a side room about twenty feet square with shelves on all the walls stacked with packets. "Look!" he waved his arms. "Look at all these proposals from companies all over the world."

As we looked, I tried to estimate the number of submission packets, some inches thick, others less than one-half inch, most about eight and a half by eleven inches in size, but other sizable stacks were larger with folded plans and engineering drawings. I was astounded at the volume of proposals, none of which had yet been opened.

Because of my education at Georgia Tech's School of Architecture and my career in real estate development, I could understand what I was seeing.

"There must be a thousand submissions here, Sheikh Ali," I exclaimed.

"And these are only during the past month, Mr. Simon. I don't know what to do with all of these submissions. We are not staffed or equipped to analyze the mountains of proposals we are receiving.

Fortunately, we have many educated Palestinians in Kuwait we hire for such things. Kuwaiti citizens today pay others to do their work for them. Palestinian engineers are among the very best. They build and operate most of our infrastructure. You see, after the World War I, the British governed Palestine and Iraq. The French occupied and governed Lebanon and Syria, and England protected us, so they and we have had the advantage of Western thinking and Western education for nearly sixty years, less in Palestine because of Israel's takeover in 1947-48. They are our brothers and so we subsidize King Hussein as does Saudi Arabia and the Emirates. And which we will do for Palestine as soon as a Palestinian state is established.

"You know, foreigners now out-populate natural Kuwaitis, who are among the richest people in the world. Everything is free for Kuwaiti citizens. And that is creating a problem. Our citizens refuse to work. They need nothing. The government provides everything. So everyone wants to be part of the government. Or simply travel and invest. Or do nothing! I don't think any Kuwaitis even fish in the Gulf anymore!

We loved his joke and laughed together.

"Yes," Sheikh Ali added, "we Kuwaitis have a very good life. Perhaps too good?"

After another cup of tea, Sheikh Ali told us of the history of Kuwait, where it came from and where it is today.

"The region that became Kuwait was first inhabited since around 2000 BC. There were several tribes, including the Al Sabah, Al Khalifah, and Al Jalahma. Pearl diving and trade were the principal occupations. The Gulf reefs from near Iraq southward to Bahrain, the island colony and Qatar, and the small peninsula south to the Emirates toward the Strait of Hormus have provided excellent pearl beds for centuries.

"The Al Sabah family found fresh water in 1716 and became quite an important family. In 1756, the Al Sabah family obtained control of the trade with Aleppo and Baghdad and assumed control of territory of the Al Khalifa leadership which was more focused on maritime trade. Their tribal members migrated south to Bahrain. Others like the Al Thani tribe went farther south to Qatar and the Emirates. My ancestor, Abdallah Al Sabah ruled Kuwait from 1762-1812.

"In 1775, the Al Sabahs established trade relations with the British East India Company. By that time, Britain had a naval and trade presence throughout much of the world, establishing trade and markets from Canada, and the American colonies in the west to India and South Asia in the east. Kuwait provided an excellent and convenient location for caravans traveling from Aleppo, Syria, Baghdad, and other Mediterranean ports to Kuwait. The British gathered these supplies and goods from all over the region in Kuwait City's port, one of the best natural harbors in the Gulf. Both countries prospered as a result of favorable terms for both. Kuwait became an important trading post for trade. The British coveted the valuable pearls Kuwaitis gathered from one of the best pearl beds in the world; horses, spices, dates and goods from Baghdad and wheat and spices from Syria, with enormous profits made here, in India, and again back in England.

"In 1899, the Germans sought to take over Kuwait. We called on Britain for help, and with that support, Kuwait established its independence, separate from Saudi Arabia and Iraq.

"In 1914, during World War I, Britain recognized Kuwait's independence and in 1923 recognized its borders with Iraq and Saudi

Arabia. Britain's imprimatur preserved Kuwait's independence despite political factions in Iraq who claimed Kuwait was truly part of Iraq. This feeling among some in Iraq persists to this day. Kuwait's very existence reduced Iraq's coast in the Gulf to a very small coastline and shipping access which many in Iraq feel deprives them from greater trade possibilities. It is possible Iraq could one day seek a military takeover of Kuwait, our oil wells, and our ports."

It seems today that his vision was quite prescient.

We learned that in 1933, oil was first discovered in Saudi Arabia by Western companies, and in 1938 oil was discovered in Kuwait. In 1963, Kuwait and Saudi Arabia agreed to cooperate in the exploration of more oil, an amicable agreement that continues to this day.

He reminded us that since early in the twentieth century, Kuwait has been allied with the West, especially Britain and the United States, as has Saudi Arabia, and that during the Cold War, neither Kuwait nor Saudi Arabia or the Emirates, with their enormous oil deposits ever traded with the Soviets, as the atheism of the Soviets was anathema to Muslims. "Not one riyal, not one ruble!"

We took part in incredibly informative meetings with other high officials in the Kuwait government, including their Minister of Oil Resources, Ministers of Intelligence, Foreign Affairs, Housing, and Communications. Later, we met the Emir of Kuwait who confirmed the same position as King Hussein regarding the ongoing negotiations between Egypt, Israel and the United States, stating that unless there is a provision for a Palestinian state, Egypt will be isolated. Kuwait, like Iraq, Jordan, Syria, and Lebanon, after all, had received hundreds of thousands of Palestinian refugees, including thousands of well-educated engineers, doctors, and technicians who actually operated most of Kuwait's infrastructure and facilities, reportedly including Yasser Arafat, a Palestinian civil engineer.

After all our meetings, the next morning we met with U.S. Embassy officials and reported what we had learned. The embassy was conveniently located just a block from the hotel. The U.S. ambassador was not in residence. We were surprised that not one staff member or the ambassador spoke Arabic.

Kuwait City: Iconic symbols, city water tanks, Persian Gulf in background. U.S. Embassy in foreground

Kuwait City: (L-R) Sandy Simon, Hisham Sharabi,
Sheikh Ali Al Sabah, Minister of Defense, Sheryl Ameen,
Joe Baroody

Camp David Accords

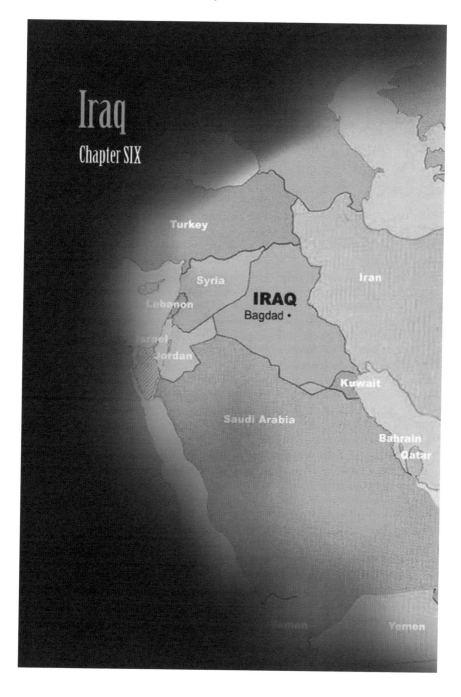

Camp David Accords

Chapter 6
Iraq

Two days after our arrival, we flew to Baghdad in order to learn and understand Iraq's position on the U.S. sponsored negotiations.

Ahh, Baghdad! Sinbad, oases, all the Hollywood images raced through my mind. Iraq, formerly Babylonia in Biblical stories. Wow! We were truly excited to be flying into Baghdad, capital of a country rich in agriculture, education, oil production, huge oil reserves, and very Western in its human rights and trade with the West. Iraq, like Jordan and Kuwait, had liberal and secular societies.

In Baghdad, we met with several high officials of the Ba'ath party and spent several hours at Baghdad University, which at that time had an enrollment of over forty thousand students, fully fifty percent young women.

Saddam Hussein, although controlling Iraq as a Strong Chairman of the Ba'ath Party and General of the Armed Forces the time, and essentially ruled Iraq did not become Iraq's president until a year following our visit. We were taken by car to the University of Baghdad. As we were guided across the beautiful and busy campus, we watched many students pass by.

"Look, Sandy," Sheryl exclaimed, "nearly all the men and women students are dressed in Western style jeans and shirts! Iraq really is secular under the Ba'ath party!"

49

"It's going to be the same in Syria," we were told.

We walked the campus, receiving overwhelming friendliness from students, faculty and visitors. Many spoke English, with maybe at the most, fewer than a dozen women wearing burkas. Iraq, definitely a secular nation, formerly under mandate as a protectorate of England after WW I, was clearly, among the population, pro-Western. Yet, we found everyone we met very much opposed to the U.S. sponsored unilateral negotiations with Israel and Egypt, again confirming what we had heard in Jordan. "There may not be another region-wide war, but there will be no peace without a Palestinian state," many told us.

Iraq, we learned, was now home to more than a half million Palestinian refugees. Iraq, adjacent to Iran, was also predominantly Shiia Muslim as is Iran. Under the Shah, a brutal despot, Iran was also a secular state, bordering on the north with the Soviet Union, yet an ally with the United States. Iran is Persian, not Arab. Their language is Farsi, not Arabic though they all are mostly Shiite Muslim

That evening, we were taken to a fine restaurant on a boat and dined while anchored on the Tigris River. The Tigris River flows through Baghdad providing more than an abundance of fresh water. The very idea of dining <u>on</u> the Tigris was pretty exciting. I think I was in the eighth grade when I first studied the Tigris and Euphrates rivers.

"This is really amazing, isn't it, Sandy," Sheryl whispered to me while Hisham, clearly a socialist, anti-royalty, was happy in Baghdad. He and our host, whom he must have known, laughed together, speaking in Arabic, then quietly telling us that Iraq and Syria, both led by their respective Ba'ath parties, were actually discussing a *"rapprochement."* We could not tell if this was considered the first step at becoming one state, or simply having both governments work closely together on all international issues. Most likely the latter. We understood later the idea collapsed when Syria's condition was that Hafez Al Assad would be president, not Saddam Hussein.

Our host saw the food being delivered to our long table, and said, *"Ahlen oo Sahlen,"* (welcome), and then *"Fuduloo,"* (honor us). Then, "Eat!"

We watched, surprised, as he reached *into* the large poached fish caught that day in the river, a large silver fish about four feet long, four inches thick, still with its head and tail, and scooped out with his hand a large serving, which he placed on Hisham's plate before serving the rest of us in the same fashion. Obviously, our cultures clashed, and as we looked for serving spoons, we smiled at each other, shrugged our shoulders, and ate our dinner … as served. One does not leave a nearly full plate, add condiments or ask for any change as they would be considered slights or insults

There were other culture differences. As Sheryl prepared for our trip, she had called me to tell me she planned on wearing boots covering her calves, long sleeved blouses, scarves to cover her hair, and long skirts. She didn't feel it necessary to bring along a head to ankle *abeyeh or burka* despite the fact that all but Jordan, Iraq, Syria, Jordan, and Lebanon, had strict dress codes for women. In fact, Sheryl went to the Islamic Center in Washington, D.C. before she left to make sure what she was taking on the trip would not be offensive to anyone, especially anyone in Saudi Arabia.

Another important cultural code includes never, never showing others the bottom of one's shoes. As a result, we always kept both feet flat on the floor during our meetings, never crossing our legs. Showing the bottom of one's shoe is considered the height of insult.

Sandy Simon with two Iraqi citizens at Baghdad souk

Baghdad, Iraq: Senate building, Ba'ath Party HQ:
(L-R) Party Official, Host, Hisham Sharabi, Director,
Ba'ath Party, Joe Baroody, Sandy Simon

Following our meetings and reporting to the U.S. Embassy staff, we were taken on a tour of Baghdad, including the magnificent Islamic Center with fabulous colorful ceramic tile mosaics seemingly everywhere and to the huge, really outstanding Souk Baghdad. We walked throughout the souk, passing hundreds of fresh food and fruit booths, unbelievable abundance of local products including succulent fresh dates still on the branches harvested from the south near Basra, a highly prolific agricultural region. Most fascinating were the hundreds of metal crafts booths. We marveled as we watched craftsmen and women tapping and configuring all kinds of polished and shiny pots, trays, samovars, bowls … some up to six feet high! Brass, copper and silver were the favored inlay metals. Of course, tempted by these unusual, rare, beautiful artifacts, we purchased several magnificent examples. I bought a beautiful brass samovar about thirty inches high. We had to restrain ourselves because we knew we had to somehow transport them back home. We coveted natural, beautiful pearls from Kuwait, Bahrain, and Qatar, brass, copper and silver from Baghdad, and wood mosaics from Syria. What a terrific shopping spree!

At the remarkable Baghdad museum, we were shown antiquities of all kinds. We especially were impressed with an eight-foot tall black obelisk on which the civil laws of Babylonia set four thousand years ago were carved in Arabic. It was made of epoxy, a copy because the original in stone was taken and is still exhibited in England. Another exhibit was a prone skeleton of a man purported to be 4,000 years old.

We hated to leave Iraq, such a beautiful and fascinating country. The people couldn't have been kinder or friendlier, from government officials to the pedestrians and crafts artisans.

I recall Hisham and his friends pointing out how wonderful it was living in a socialist country, secular, and relatively free.

But we saw many, many very poor people, some pushing wagons of food, carrying their goods on their backs. Clearly, many were not enjoying the "good life" as political leaders everywhere in this socialist nation where Adam Smith's "Invisible Hand" doesn't seem to spread the wealth to the poor.

At the end of our meetings, we left the government center, guarded by several heavily armed soldiers with automatic assault weapons, and entered our black, stretch government limousine. After we sat inside, I smiled as I said to Hisham, "I do love a country where everyone is indeed equal."

But, as I noticed a poor citizen push his wagon through the muddy street, I said, "Isn't it wonderful that we and the government people are just a little more equal than everyone else?"

Hisham didn't appreciate my little joke. But I kept my smile.

Baghdad Souk: Artisan at work

Camp David Accords

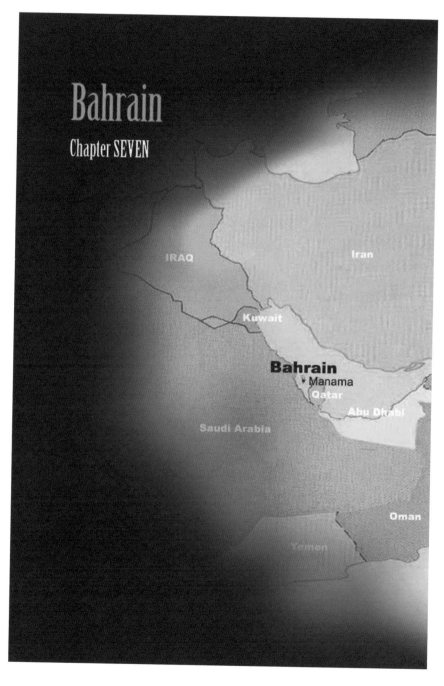

Bahrain
Chapter SEVEN

Camp David Accords

Chapter 7
Bahrain

From Baghdad, we flew to Manama, Bahrain, a small predominantly Shiite Muslim Persian Gulf island kingdom offshore from Saudi Arabia, but not far from Iran to the east. The ruling family is Sunni, which could in the future eventually create problems. The difference between the Sunnis and Shiites is mostly political rather than questions of theology. The majority of Muslims are Sunni making up 85 percent throughout the world.

As we drove into the city from the airport, we were impressed with the substantial construction of housing taking place. We toured the island with the Minister of Housing who explained that the government utilizes its new vast oil receipts for building housing, hospitals, schools, infrastructure, roads, utilities, and improvements to its ports. The population, he explained, was principally Shiite Muslim. The ruling family government is Sunni Muslim.

We also met with the Foreign Minister who described Bahrain's strong opposition to the negotiations between Israel and Egypt. "An independent Palestinian state is vital to the region. Without that, we will live with instability for many, many years, perhaps more than thirty years. (Note: as of this writing, it has been 35 years.) The absence of provision for a Palestinian state will keep Bahrain and all the other Arab

59

countries from joining Egypt. Anwar Sadat will be alone, a pariah, unless he delivers a Palestinian state. But we do not believe Israel's Menachem Begin and his extremist Likud Party will ever honestly consider a Palestinian state that even if approved, would occupy just the West Bank and perhaps Gaza, just twenty percent of what was Palestine. And, we know that only with America's enormous financial and military support can Israel stand rigid, not agreeing to a Palestinian state.

"We in Bahrain have accepted tens of thousands of Palestinian refugees. Many are our technocrats as they are so well educated in the sciences. And many came as penniless refugees.

"Their families are now very much a part of our population and economy. It has not been very long since Bahrain's income came mostly from pearl diving. Now, we have substantial oil revenues with which we are building colleges, infrastructure, hospitals, and utility facilities, but we need the Palestinians to operate them for us."

Finally, we met the Emir Al Khalifa. He could not have been more gracious, hospitable, friendlier, and more candid with us. Bright and aware of the world's issues, our visit with this diminutive king was a highlight of our trip. Immediately on our arrival, another servant brought the beautifully embossed silver teapot with the Eastern-styled curved spout together with very small cups stacked in his left hand, and offered each of us a cup of local yellow tea. One sip was enough for me, but I knew if I didn't accept a refill I would insult the Emir. A slight dilemma, drinking more of something that to me tasted awful was a test of my wanting to be respectful. Discretion overcame taste! I smiled at Joe and Sheryl. I remember being surprised that the Emir smoked Winston cigarettes and when he wanted to smoke, he made a subtle signal with a slight movement of his right hand, and immediately one of his staff came to him with a beautiful, mosaic wood box of cigarettes. He directed his staff member to offer cigarettes to his guests then drew his from the box. We accepted the cigarettes. The Emir himself then drew his Winston and lit his, and then, surprisingly, the Emir offered to light ours as well.

Our visit was most cordial and informative, reinforcing what we had already learned. Even though tiny Bahrain is geographically far from the Arab-Israeli conflicts, it still was populated by Arabs and Muslims and thus considered themselves brothers of Palestinians and aligned with the other states we had visited.

"Sadat can only negotiate a treaty that would return Egypt's Sinai. Nothing else. His efforts are all wrong. We cannot join him. We fear that as a result of America's unlimited support for Israel and Israel's extremist Zionist unwillingness to accept a Palestinian state, that many young Arabs are feeling a growing intense sense of hatred toward America."

As I looked around the high-ceilinged room, I marveled at the magnificent, opulent décor. Oriental rugs covered the entire floor. The furnishings were beautiful and tasteful, even to Westerners. The hanging tapestries on the walls and the damask covered furniture were exquisite. What a delight!

After two hours with the Emir, we left after taking photographs. Each of us embraced the short, pleasant king as he embraced us, kissing each cheek. Somehow, I think I saw his embrace of lovely Sheryl linger as he smiled.

Foreign Ministry host in Bahrain and Sandy Simon, Sr. VP
NAAA

Dhows (pearl diving boats) Persian Gulf, Bahrain

Emir of Bahrain Al Thani with Sheryl Ameen

Camp David Accords

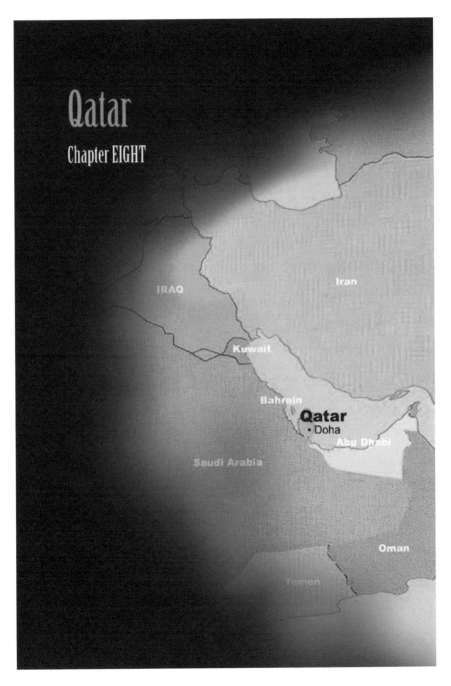

Qatar

Chapter EIGHT

Camp David Accords

Chapter 8
Qatar

It was a short flight from Manama to Doha, the capital of Qatar, a small peninsula jutting out from the east coast of Saudi Arabia into the Gulf. The Al Khalifa tribe had settled in Qatar in the 1700s, and for centuries thrived on fishing and pearl diving, but with the recent discovery of oil and even more natural gas, Qatar had become very wealthy. Since the price of oil had increased to $19.00 per barrel in 1973, billions were being spent building infrastructure and expanding the emirate by hiring Dutch companies who were expert at recovering land from the sea in Holland and elsewhere. It appeared the country intended to recover what looked like miles of more land from the Gulf thus sizably expanding the size of Qatar, and preparing for what would become an enormous modern urban financial, trading and resort center. We could see in the far distance an enormous amount of new land stretching, it seemed, miles into the Gulf. Far in the distance, a multi-storied pyramid form of construction steel rose into the sky; the skeleton of what would become an enormous Sheraton Hotel, the first of what would become a veritable new city of skyscrapers, hotels, and resorts.

The beautiful three-story palace was bright white surrounded by a contrasting huge, green lawn with trees here and there, all watered by hand, creating employment.

We learned that Qatar officials had visions of becoming an important commercial banking and trading center. They told us that due to their geographic location midway between Asia and the West, and free of conflict, they believed they could challenge Beirut as the financial center of the Middle East.

"It will take several decades," we were told by the Minister of the Interior, "but as long as we can sell our oil and natural gas at a fair price, we will bring Qatar from the fourteenth century with clay huts into the twentieth century and beyond. We have many ambitious plans."

That afternoon, following our meeting with other government officials, we were driven to the lovely, modest home of U.S. Ambassador and Mrs. Andrew Killgore, a most hospitable couple, we were told. A cheery, tall, silver-haired gentleman opened the door with his smiling wife Marjorie standing beside him.

"Well, hi, y'all! Welcome!" Marjorie exclaimed with her broad smile and strong Southern accent hanging in the air. Our first few seconds facing each other were like being home. For the previous four years I lived in Newnan, Georgia, a small town thirty miles southwest of Atlanta, just twenty miles from Alabama.

Ambassador Andrew Killgore

"Hello," I replied with a Southern accent, and venturing a guess, I asked, "are you two from Alabama?"

"We sure are," Marjorie happily replied. "Why don't y'all come on in and make yourselves comfortable?" she said, leading us into their comfortably furnished living room.

Indeed, they were most hospitable, gracious, and welcoming. In just a few minutes, Marjorie was offering us a tray glasses of water, cups of tea and orange juice, reflecting the culture of the Arab world, i.e., invite one's guests to get comfortable, sit, chat, offer beverages of cups of hot tea, juice, and water before discussing important matters.

After Hisham introduced us and explained our mission, he told the ambassador where we had been and what we had heard.

Ambassador Killgore smiled and said, "Call us Andy and Marjorie. We're Americans just like you and we're surely from Alabama!"

We enjoyed several hours becoming acquainted, and quite informed, mostly regarding the Gulf States, the Arab United Emirates and the region as a whole in a very friendly and relaxed atmosphere.

Andy and I spoke about Alabama, Georgia, Southern ethics, President Carter's heritage in South Georgia, and then I asked, "How in the world did you two find yourselves in Doha, Qatar, so far from Alabama?"

The ambassador laughed and said, "We surely are a long way from Alabama, but I've been in the Foreign Service a long time, and I think I'm one of the few diplomats in the Arab world who speaks fluent Arabic. Some people in the State Department consider anyone who speaks fluent Arabic to be an 'Arabist' and therefore 'anti-Israel,' which is a stupid logic. But those of us career diplomats who speak Arabic find ourselves sent by the State Department as far away as possible," he laughed, "and Qatar is really far away!"

Then Marjorie added, in her deep Southern accent, "The people of Qatar are really so friendly, we do love it here. It's almost like being in Alabama."

The ambassador continued, "I really like the people here and they've been good to us. They have great respect for America, and many young men attend the best colleges in the U.S. I think Qatar has a great future."

As an excellent career diplomat for the United States, Ambassador Killgore had established warm relations with many members of the royal family, the Al Thani, who had been the ruling family since the mid-1800s.

He told us many things about Qatar, a nation of about 300,000, mostly Shiite Muslims. Years ago, Qatar, like Bahrain and Kuwait, established strong trading ties with Great Britain and, with its support, achieved independence in 1971. And with that independence, under the Emir Khalifa bin Hamad Al Thani, there was significant progress toward development, modernization, international relations, modern schools and curricula, housing, jobs, and greatly expanded oil and gas production. We also learned that young members of the very large royal family had been sent to study in Great Britain and the United States. The ambassador commented that they would return with different, global views of the world. "Many get undergraduate degrees but many more stay to obtain their Masters degrees or MBAs from the finest schools like Princeton, Yale, Stanford, Harvard, Wharton, and other schools with top reputations. As a result," he added, "Qatar, along with the other Arab oil producing nations, will soon become more involved in international relations and not remain so parochial in their nature."

Much of what Ambassador Killgore told us helped us understand the varied differences between the smaller emirates in the Persian Gulf and those Arab states on the Mediterranean Sea. The Gulf Emirates nonetheless voiced full support of the positions of the other Arab states. That is, strongly opposing the unilateral negotiations between Egypt and Israel. Their universal belief remained the same: Israel governed by the extremist Likud Party would likely never agree under any conditions to accept a Palestinian state on the West Bank, the remaining twenty percent of Palestine, and that U.S. politics would not challenge Israel's position. As a result a stalemate of twenty-one Arab states was solidly unified in their opposition to the soon to be labeled "Camp David Peace Accords."

"There really needs to be a regional peace agreement including Syria, Palestine, Lebanon, Jordan, and Egypt, not just one Arab country. The Arabs feel it would be like only England signing a peace agreement with Germany after World War II. I mean, what would that mean for France, the Baltics, and the U.S.?"

After a wonderful two days in Qatar, meeting with so many government officials, understanding its history, culture and mores, it was time for us to bid adieu to our new friends, especially Andy and Marjorie Killgore, who, indeed, served us a delightful meal of grits (from Alabama) and shrimp from Qatar's waters.

Saudi Arabia

Chapter NINE

Camp David Accords

Chapter 9
Saudi Arabia

Back on the Alia Airlines Lear jet, we flew to Riyadh, Saudi Arabia. En route we could see miles and miles of desert sands, dunes, and, on occasion, oil rigs, sometimes with flames leaping into the sky, burning off the excess escaping gases.

Finally, we approached Riyadh, a booming city in the desert. It was a time of large scale construction, unlike in the West, which was in the middle of a severe recession. There were so many construction cranes at construction sites of high office buildings, apartment buildings, and condominiums that they jokingly called the construction crane the "national bird."

The only large green areas we could see in the entire city were what appeared to be a camel racetrack and soccer fields with artificial green grass. We marveled at the aerial view of the capital of Saudi Arabia with its tree-lined boulevards, sand colored buildings, and busy traffic. We were filled with anticipation of our upcoming meetings with King Khalid, Ibn Saud Abdul Aziz, Prince Turki bin Faisal Ibn Saud, and other high officials. Saudi Arabia was the wealthiest of all countries with the largest known oil reserves in the world. The oil could be extracted from the earth quite inexpensively, which provided enormous economic leverage. They had for decades used this judiciously after great deliberation. Saudi Arabia too was the keeper of the sacred Islam

75

sites of Medina and Mecca. Now, with Jerusalem considered one of Islam's holiest sites, and taken by the Israelis in 1967, we already believed the Saudi government would not participate in the Egyptian-Israeli Accords without East Jerusalem being returned to the Arabs.

Soon after we landed, we were taken to the beautiful, new Sheraton Hotel located adjacent to the huge, very tastefully designed conference center. Both were constructed of sandstone, the light ochre color of the dunes we had viewed. After we registered for our rooms in the elegant hotel, each of us went to our respective rooms, showered, and met for dinner in the hotel dining room. Again, we were served orange juice and hot tea. Of course, no liquor was available or apparent, as Islam prohibits the imbibing of such things.

After dinner, we retired, each alone with our private thoughts of what was to come during our scheduled meetings.

The next morning, as I dressed, I realized that I didn't have my wallet. *Oh, Lord, I thought, what am I going to do without my wallet, my money and my identification? And with us yet to visit Syria and Lebanon?*

I quickly reached for the phone and called the front desk.

"Good morning, Mr. Simon," the voice said in English with a Middle Eastern accent. "How can I help you?"

"I've lost my wallet, sir. Can you help me find it?"

"Of course, sir. Do not worry." Then, after a couple of moments, he returned to the telephone and asked, "Is your wallet brown leather, folded for your rear pocket?"

"Yes, it is!"

"Well, Mr. Simon, here it is on our counter, exactly where you left it yesterday when you registered."

"You mean it's still on the counter?"

"Yes, sir. You need not worry about theft here at the Sheraton, nor, I must add, should you worry about theft in Riyadh. It simply doesn't happen!"

"Well," I said, "my wallet would have disappeared in just a few minutes in New York or any other large city in the U.S.!" We both laughed, and I quickly took the elevator down to the lobby and retrieved my wallet. I checked the wallet, and sure enough, everything was intact. *What a nice culture,* I thought.

Riyadh, Saudi Arabia: Convention Center adjacent to
Sheraton Hotel

Most of our first day was spent meeting with high government and royal family officials, including the impressive Prince Turki bin Faisal, Minister of Intelligence, a tall, handsome member of the royal family, who was educated in the U.S. at Princeton, and held a Master's degree in economics. He was so aware of America, the world, and Saudi Arabia's place in the world, principally because of its enormous oil reserves, its worldwide philanthropy, large and growing investments in Europe and the U.S., and its desire to keep the price of oil reasonable so that the economies of the West would function successfully. (Note: Prince Turki later became ambassador to the U.S., and later Foreign Minister.)

"A robust world economy is in the best interests of my country. We have been an ally and good friend of America ever since my grandfather promised President Franklin Roosevelt during World War II an unlimited supply of crude oil at low prices. We have fulfilled that promise ever since. Throughout the Cold War, Saudi Arabia never traded even one riyal with the Soviet Union or the Soviet's eastern bloc. We have enormous investments in Western Europe and in the United States. We are one of your most trusted friends. In addition, our sizeable purchases from America create millions of American jobs.

"However," he continued, "these current negotiations between Israel and Egypt are problematic for us. There must be a provision for a Palestinian state or Egypt will be alone for many years even though they are the largest and most populated Arab country. But we are convinced, despite America's significant investment in these negotiations that Israel, especially under the hardline, unreasonable Likud Party led by Mr. Begin, will never agree to a Palestinian state. And thus, we see no reason to be involved in any way. And we will not without an overall regional settlement. The Palestinians must have their human rights restored and they must have their own state."

Then, he stepped to a large globe of the world and invited us to gather around it, next to him. He slowly spun the globe so that the United States and the Western hemisphere were on top, virtually all we could see.

"You see?" he asked. "If you are an American, you cannot even see the Middle East. You cannot see Saudi Arabia. So, using this as a metaphor, we are not visible or present in the consciousness of the typical American. In the same way, with the United States so favoring Israel, the typical Saudi citizen does not consciously think about the United States each day. It is the same for both, you see?"

Riyadhi: Hisham Sharabi with bin Abdul Aziz, Minister of Intelligence

We were very impressed by the Minister and his wisdom, feeling sure he would rise in the royal family's hierarchy and become even more important.

As the four of us discussed later, he could possibly become Foreign Minister, Prime Minister, or maybe even king one day. He was most impressive.

Later, we met with the Minister of Oil Production, the Minister of Foreign Affairs, the Minister of Housing, and the Minister of Public Affairs. All were gracious and candid in their comments. One even commented that personally, he told us in a whispering voice, "The Palestinian young men are doing more harm to their cause than helping their own interests. They should act peaceably and try not to harden the angst of the Israelis."

Their views on the Egypt-Israel negotiations were near echoes to those we heard from Prince Turki, and other leaders we had met with.

Each meeting throughout our mission began with enthusiastic welcomes, warm embraces, cheek kisses, and several moments of casual discussion during which we were offered orange juice, hot tea of a variety of tastes, water, and, on one occasion, glasses of Coca-Cola. Meeting with royalty so often, and being treated as royalty, made every meeting meaningful, cordial, and informative in many dimensions from the highest authorities. We wondered why the U.S. government was biased against the Arab world, especially with the oil producing states like Saudi Arabia, Kuwait, and the Gulf Emirates, and with Lebanon, which felt so close to America.

They all were so friendly to us, forthcoming, and continually reiterated their alliance with America. After speaking with Ambassador Killgore, it did not surprise us that of the eight countries we visited, only three career ambassadors and/or staff representing the U.S. could speak Arabic. Despite this valuable talent, they were considered "Arabists" and, in some State Department quarters, therefore, incorrectly deemed anti-Israel, a real anathema to one's career advancement in Washington. Sad but true, because advancing U.S. interests is the mission of our embassies, their employees, and the value of speaking and understanding our host's language is much enhanced, and the hosts appreciate that talent, no matter where in the world.

A question asked of us several times was, "When do you think the U.S. will act in its own best interests in the Middle East?"

That night, at dinner, our group exchanged our observations. We knew Saudi Arabia had the greatest leverage of other Arab nations because it had such great wealth, oil reserves, and was generous to many poor countries, especially King Hussein's Jordan. King Hussein, believed to be a direct descendant of Mohammed, had credentials, wisdom, and vision. But, as a country adjacent to Israel, he and his country suffered greatly during any confrontation. His country absorbed hundreds of thousands of Palestinian refugees in 1947-48, and again during the 1967 war, when Jordan had to deal with additional influxes of poor refugees, creating enormous and concomitant economic and social burdens. "We are brothers," was the reply when we asked why Saudi Arabia was so generous. "Oil is a blessing from God we must share. The Palestinians, the Jordanians, even the Syrians, are our brothers. And when other countries like Iran or Venezuela raise their prices too high and America is negatively impacted, we are able to and do increase our production to lower world oil prices."

As we listened to the Saudi opinions of the plight of the Palestinian people, it seemed to us that the Palestinians were analogous to the Native American tribes in the Americas when the Europeans arrived finding generous, friendly natives, but considered them "savages" because they looked different, dressed differently, and seemed "Godless infidels" to the European Christian colonists. As a result, the Indians were considered lower than humans, and taking their land became justified. And this, we came to believe, was the Israelis' justification for taking land owned and occupied by the Palestinians. First they stereotyped, then labeled the indigenous people cockroaches and terrorists.

We also became quite aware that the memories of the Western Invasion, known in the West as the Crusades, some nine hundred years earlier were still deep in the minds of many Arabs and considered the huge influx of Europeans into Palestine following the brutal Holocaust thrust on the Jews of Europe by the Nazis. Many became angry, feeling Israel's creation to be a repeat of that invasion from the West in an effort to take Arab land, destroy their culture, and threaten their religion.

"It was the European Christians who invaded and took our land before. Now, the European Jews have come and taken Palestine."

These were clearly deep-rooted, problematic issues that should and could be resolved. The Saudis, like the others, were insistent on the creation of a Palestinian state as a condition of peace with Israel. "But if Israel insists on staying in the West Bank, the Golan, Gaza and East Jerusalem there can be no peace in the Middle East.

Hisham said to us, "Tomorrow, God willing, *Inshallah*, we will meet with the King of Saudi Arabia."

We were all very excited with this very important personal meeting. "Tomorrow then, before noon."

* * * * *

The next morning, about ten a.m., after breakfast and a brief return to my room, I stepped out onto the mezzanine overlooking the lobby. I was surprised to see Hisham and Joe Baroody together, walking out the front doors.

"Where are you going without Sheryl and me?" I called out to them.

Hisham turned, looked up at me and exclaimed, "We are going to meet with King Khalid."

"Without Sheryl and me?" I yelled. Then, in an angry, loud statement, I said sternly, "Do not walk out that door without us or I will be" (I thought appropriately to say) royally pissed! You cannot leave here without us!" They didn't leave.

"Then hurry down," Hisham replied. "We're running late. And don't bring Sheryl. The King will not meet with a woman!"

"What?" I didn't believe that was true, but rather Hisham's assumption. I turned to Sheryl's room to get her. She wasn't completely ready, but I told her what Hisham told me. She immediately got both angry and sad. "I don't believe that, Sandy. But you go. I'll stay here."

I hated to leave Sheryl, but Hisham made all our appointments and was in charge, so I raced down to join the two I'd been traveling with for nine days. A very sad and hurt Sheryl wasn't part of our delegation for the first time. And I was very disappointed for her. Later I was told the king's staff thought Sheryl was simply our group's secretary and not an officer.

We were driven in a limousine by a member of the King's staff to the Royal Palace, a magnificent, regal edifice, and were led by another staff member into a very large, high-ceilinged room with large Oriental carpets covering nearly every square foot of floor. To me, the design was warm and beautiful, constructed of sand-colored sandstone. It was at one moment, a thrill to think we would be meeting with King Khalid himself, but I couldn't help feeling sad that Sheryl wasn't with us.

As we looked around the large room, we saw several tall men in brown *dishdash* gowns, standing ready for any event. Unarmed, they were present for any request from the king. As is Arab custom, all chairs were lined against all three walls (the fourth was open to connect with other meeting rooms) so all can see each other face to face, rather than in rows or around a table or on couches in a living room setting. My good fortune continued as I was led to the chair that would be on the king's left, our chairs literally touching each other. I was, I confess, thrilled at this unexpected honor. Hisham, as president of NAAA, sat to the king's right. And, of course, Hisham was multi-lingual and conversed in both languages with the king. In just a moment, as King Khalid entered the room, we stood in respect and as he approached, he extended an embrace to each of us in a hug with kisses on our cheeks.

"It is wonderful being here with you, Your Majesty," I

86

whispered.

As the king whispered to me, "Thank you, we are honored with your presence," I could see he was impressively regal with his black goatee, elegantly attired in his *dishdash* (loose fitting gown) and kiffeyeh (headdress), topped with his *aghal* (black rope circled on top), and exquisite English-made brown wool cloak, elegantly trimmed with gold threaded in a band about an inch wide along the entire front edges and collar.

How I wished I had my camera, yet, it's a moment I never forgot.

The king then stepped to his chair, which was slightly larger than ours, its back slightly taller, and sat down. After a slight gesture by the king, we then followed his lead and also sat in our chairs, Hisham's on his right, mine on his left, touching his, now positioned to converse with King Khalid. He turned to me and then welcomed us with a warm smile. "You are our brothers and we are very happy to see you here today."

Surprisingly, he spoke in English having studied in England and the U.S. we later learned, and with keen interest, asked about our mission. Hisham then described to him our mission for President Carter, where we had been and with whom we had met.

The king then turned to me and asked where we would go after meeting with him. I replied, "We next fly to Damascus to meet with President Hafez Al Assad, and after Syria, to Beirut to meet with President Elias Sarkis." Then, I added, "We hope to meet with Chairman Yassir Arafat in Beirut as well."

King Khalid got right to the point as he spoke to us about his love for America and the American people. "Your government appears to have turned its back on its best allies in the Middle East. We have been loyal friends since my father met with your President Roosevelt in the early 1930s. We do not understand why America supports so generously the State of Israel as it treats the Palestinian people so terribly. Why do they support the taking of the Palestinian homes, their farms, and their land? And now, they allow Mr. Begin to dictate terms of their agreement and induce Egypt into signing a peace treaty with Israel without including a secure homeland for the Palestinian people.

"Of course," he added, "we in Saudi Arabia cannot sign such an agreement without provision for Palestinian human rights, a Palestinian homeland, and return of East Jerusalem, and will be forced to reject such an agreement. I hope you will take that message back to President Carter."

Then, with a slight wave of his hand, one of his service staff (they reminded me of Mumluk warriors in their tan-grey *dishdash* gowns, came toward us with a large silver teapot with its curved spout.

"Would you join me for a cup of tea?" the king inquired. We nodded of course.

Each of us was delivered a tiny cup from the stack of cups in the waiter's left hand as he offered each of us a cup and filled it with a grey-looking, unfamiliar to us, cup of tea. I must confess, it didn't taste good, but if we didn't drink it, it would have been considered an insult. Yet, when we drank the tea, the waiter hastened to refill our cups almost instantly. Another cultural dilemma!

"How can we help you, Your Majesty?" I asked. "We need to

work with you to improve the image of Saudi Arabia in America. Perhaps your government could send emissaries to America to promote goodwill between Saudi Arabia and the American people, or, perhaps begin student exchange programs so that young Americans can see your country personally. And young Saudis could see the United States and meet young Americans."

"That is a good idea. Our cause is just," he replied. "We want to be America's friend. We have done all we can to provide the necessary oil from our soil to keep the Western economies successful, and we prefer purchasing U.S. products. We have never traded with the Soviet Union. But you must understand that the Muslim world cannot stand by silently forever as we watch Israel treat our brothers so badly. That is why we have ceased communication with America since these negotiations, which will bear no fruit for our suffering brothers and sisters in Palestine at the hands of the Israelis.

"Some young Saudis, as throughout the Arab world, are growing very angry at America. It is difficult to determine what they will do. But it won't be good for the United States or for us."

He added, "I am concerned the young people of the Arab world will rise up one day and become a dangerous adversary of the United States, its allies and its partner Israel. We must work together to prevent this. Do you understand what I am saying?"

I felt a strong sense of foreboding from the King, telling us he was deeply concerned that the U.S.-Israel alliance and even West-leaning Arab governments were starting to be considered the enemies of Muslims — that young extremists were deeply angry at the United States and may undertake means of revenge against American interests.

I wasn't sure what that really meant, but on September 11, 2001, I recalled his prescience.

Then, the King said to me, "We believe if Egypt alone signs a peace agreement with Israel without the establishment of a Palestinian state; there likely may be no more regional wars. But," he added, "there will also be no peace, no peace for the Palestinians, Syrians, Lebanese and certainly, no peace for the Israelis. There is great anger at the Israelis taking of all of Palestine, their treatment of Palestinians' human rights, and America's total support of Israel's terrible behavior.

"Saudi Arabia wants peace throughout the region. With America's commitment to Israel, we acknowledge that state exists. We would support a regional peace treaty with Israel. And the entire Arab world would establish peace with Israel but only if they return to their 1967 borders, which means the return of East Jerusalem, the West Bank, the Golan to Syria, Gaza and Egyptian lands."

I couldn't believe the impact of his words: *We would support a peace treaty with Israel and throughout the Middle East!* Surely if Saudi Arabia offered such a peace proposal, all Arab countries would follow. Even Syria! It seemed to us that if Israel truly wanted peace and security, they too would agree to these terms, the Saudis and the entire Arab world would, including Israel's security. What an inspiring message we can take back with us. Several years later, such a proposal from Saudi Arabia and the Arab world was presented to the U.S. and Israel. Again, Israel rejected that regional peace proposal

The king continued, "You are very welcome here because you are brothers to us."

"Thank you, Your Majesty," I replied with a slight, respectful nod of my head. "You have been very forthright, kind, and gracious. It is important that Saudi Arabia and the United States remain close allies for benefit of the world economy and security of the free world."

For the second hour, still sitting next to King Khalid, we witnessed the arrival, one by one, of Saudi citizens, humbly approach the King, bow, and softly offer to him their grievances to which he listened intently. After each, he signaled an assistant to approach and with his assent, resolve the problem for each and every petitioner, handing him a note of instructions.

I was reminded by his personal accessibility how impossible it is in America to approach our president, or even our senators or congressmen.

We were all impressed with the accessibility of King Khalid, "keeper of the holy sites of Islam," king of a country with the world's largest known oil reserves. I was astounded watching what appeared to be a ritual we later were informed was a weekly event.

Before we left, after our three hours with King Khalid, I urged him to consider a public relations effort in the U.S. to convince the American people that Saudi Arabia was indeed its friend. He quickly replied again, "Our cause is just. God will provide."

"But, Your Majesty," I dared, "even God sent a Messenger," fully knowing a "Messenger" from God was the title given Mohammed. I followed with, "The pro-Israeli allies in America spend millions to lobby our senators and congressmen for their allegiance."

"Yes, we understand most of your politicians have been induced to support Israel, right or wrong."

As we stood to leave the King, and having already met with his ministers, we were prepared to leave for our next stop: Damascus.

"Tell President Assad, when you are in Damascus, to work harder to build a better image for Syria in America." Then, he smiled, embraced each of us, kissing both cheeks, following the Arab culture of fellowship and grace.

Now, we had to move on to meet with Syrian officials, President Assad, and U.S. Ambassador Talcott Seelye.

* * * * *

Throughout the two and one half hour flight on our small but wonderful Alia Airlines Lear jet, Sheryl, Joe and I discussed the findings of our trip to date. Because of the continual negative images of the Arab people on U.S. media, I must admit we were a bit surprised with the warm hospitality of our hosts, the people of the Arab world and especially of the heads of state who most eagerly wanted to meet with and convey their views to the highest levels of the government of the United States. They manifested the warmth and grace we all had grown up with as first generation Arab-Americans. We too, like they, couldn't understand the negative attitudes of our government and media toward the Arab people.

Certainly, we were convinced that the Arabs, their leadership and public admired the United States, the American people, and wished for better, warmer relationships. It became clear that the only obstacle to warmer relations between governments was the significant imbalance of the United States government favoring Israel and Israel's treatment of the Palestinian people and taking of their lands.

The message we received at every stop was: "We have no animosity to the Jewish people at all. They are our cousins, we respect their ancient religion, because after all, they follow the one true god as we do and much of the Koran is predicated on Judaism. But the Zionists are different. They insist only on taking more and more land for Jews only no matter who is killed, robbed and even slaughtered. We do not consider all Jews as Zionists. But, we do resent and oppose the actions of the hardline Zionist State of Israel led by the Likud Party, a very harsh government toward its neighbors, especially the Palestinian people. And until the human rights of the Palestinians are restored and a Palestinian state established, we will stand fast against the Zionists. We simply cannot understand nor accept the current position of America's imbalanced enormous financial and military support of Israel's terrible treatment of the Palestinians."

Camp David Accords

.

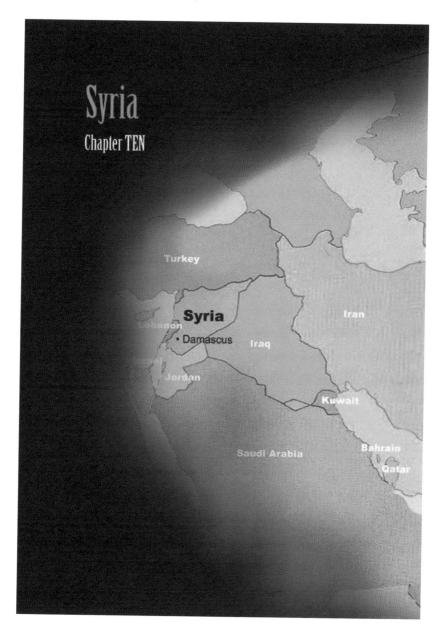

Syria

Chapter TEN

Camp David Accords

Chapter 10
Syria I

We found it fascinating that in each city we were told, "You will find the food more to your liking and familiarity to what you have eaten all your lives when you dine in Syria and Lebanon. And you will find anything you desire at the souk in Damascus."

I was anxious to arrive in Damascus, "the jewel of the Arab world," as it is known. Sheryl too was excited to arrive in Damascus as she had already visited the city and had a wonderful opinion of the people and the incredible souk.

The city of Damascus was especially dear to me because my mother was born there and I still had many cousins living there. My mother, her parents and her slightly older sister Julia, emigrated to America in 1905 while my mother was a babe in arms and settled in Boston. Later, I learned that the predominant Lebanese/Syrian Americans (perhaps 90 percent) were Christians of the Antiochan Orthodox Church, the first church created by St. Peter, St. Paul, and St. Matthew. Her father, my grandfather, was literate and well-educated. He became a priest soon after settling in Boston. That is why I was baptized into the Antiochan Orthodox Church.

During my early years, we ate "Syrian" bread (now, called pita bread in the United States) and other Syrian foods like hummus, tabouli, koosa (stuffed squash), kibbee, and very tasty desserts like

97

baklava, cooked and baked by my mother, Aunt Julia, and my grandmother, "Sitty." I always shared my Syrian foods with my friends and classmates who looked forward to my return from lunchtime as much as I did.

But somehow, after the end of World War II and the Arab-Israeli conflict from 1947-48, it became unpopular in America to be of Syrian heritage. It later became reinforced during the Cold War as Syria, refused by the West, became a recipient of aid from the Soviet Union, as did Egypt. America had later become allied with Israel, as President Harry Truman declared recognition of the State of Israel (just fifteen minutes after Israel's main founder and Prime Minister David Ben-Gurion announced its creation), and began being funded by the West following several years of military aid from the Soviet bloc. During Lyndon Johnson's presidency, government agencies, Congress, the Senate, and media reporting of events in the Middle East changed and the imbalance became extreme. Syria and Egypt both became pariahs in the United States. So, most of my Syrian or Lebanese friends and relatives, all Christians whose families came from Syria and Lebanon, then declared themselves (including me), as "Lebanese Americans." I was justified because my father and paternal grandfather emigrated to America from northern Lebanon, then a Christian country, which, at the time of its independence as a state in 1943, was no longer a province of Syria. At that time, the majority, about 60 percent, was Christian, mostly Maronite Catholic and Antiochan Orthodox (the same as Greek and Russian Orthodox).

* * * * *

As we neared Damascus, Sheryl and I shared our enthusiasm of our impending visit. She had visited Damascus earlier with her family, but this would be my first visit to this major metropolitan city, a city of about six million that was both east and west in culture as France occupied Lebanon and Syria after World War II. Both were secular nations under President Hafez Al Assad and the Ba'ath Party, as was Iraq, and enjoyed a long and strong history of freedom of religion, free enterprise, a democratic republic where minorities were safe. Assad, a member of the Alawite sect, a branch of Shiite Islam in a nation predominantly Sunni Muslim, had become president in a coup following the humiliating 1967 Six-Day War eleven years earlier. Israel had caught everyone by surprise and captured Syria's Golan Heights (a significant source of water, fertile soil, and snow melt that remains a major source of water that replenishes the Sea of Galilee and thus coveted by Israel. As a result, Syria remained a "Confrontation State" still at war with Israel, and as an ally/recipient of Soviet arms and aid, was on the opposite side from the United States during the long Cold War with the Soviet Union.

In only a few minutes, our wheels touched the tarmac and we taxied to a small, one-story welcome terminal where we were met by Issa Awad from the Ministry of Immigrants, Industry and Ministry of Foreign Affairs, and by Hisham Kahaleh, of the Protocol Department of Foreign Affairs, who welcomed us with smiles and open arms.

The date was December 19, 1978, about three months after the signing of the Camp David Accords.

We could see snow-capped Mount Hermon in the distance to the west of the city. The terrain around Damascus is flat and fertile to the east and south, bounded by mountains immediately to the north and high mountains to the west, the boundary with Lebanon.

Soon after we landed at the Damascus airport, delivered our bags and headed for our hotel, Sheryl eagerly said to me, "Let's go to the souk before our 5:30 meeting with Ambassador Talcott Seelye at the embassy."

"I'm with you! Let's do it," I happily replied.

"You are going to love Damascus, Sandy!" she laughed excitedly.

"My mother gave me an address of my cousins in Damascus," I told her. "I want to meet my cousins too!"

Syria, we had found in our research, was a veritable "breadbasket" that was part of the "fertile crescent," the source of foods for the eastern provinces of the Roman Empire some two thousand years ago. Wheat, olives, and many other food stuffs were prolific in Syrian plains and valleys, with northern and central lands providing wheat, vegetables, fruits, vineyards, and nuts. Syria had, at that time little crude oil production, only enough for their own consumption. Later more oil was discovered and today they are able to export oil along with wheat, nuts, fruit and other foods.

The Mediterranean coast provides the warm-water access the Soviets desired. Syria has a major port, Latakia, on the eastern Mediterranean Sea. This and the common Orthodox Christian religion are among the reasons Syria became a favored client state of the USSR. Russia had coveted warm water access on the Mediterranean for centuries.

Damascus' reputation as the longest continually inhabited city in the world for more than three thousand years, sits on an enormous aquifer of water that would sustain significant growth in population for decades to come. After World War II, Syria and Lebanon became occupied as a protectorate by France and thus had significant Western cultural mores blended with its eastern history and culture. It had, for centuries, been a major trading center serving the Western nations of Europe and the eastern nations of Asia.

For four hundred years it was the political center of the Mediterranean Provinces under the Ottoman Empire.

My mother's grandfather, we were told, was a wealthy trader and owner of Arabian horses, sheep, and goats. He rode his favorite horse, it was said, until his 105th birthday. He outlived three wives and ultimately passed away when he was 115 years old. I was told by my mother, "He must have eaten *laban,* yogurt with live cultures, every day of his life."

Damascus, Syria: With U.S. Ambassador Talcott Seelye
(L-R) Joe Baroody, Hasham Sharabi, Sheryl Ameen,
Ambassador Seelye

As we drove into the city, we passed tree-lined boulevards; most of the trees we saw were without leaves for the winter, although many beautiful evergreens and pines filled parks on either side. We excitedly viewed many farms, pistachio groves, and shepherds with their large and small flocks, stretching for miles into the desert. As we neared the city, we sadly witnessed the Palestinian refugee camps. They were so painful to see. As we then passed an enormous cluster of multi-storied buildings of stark unpainted concrete design surrounded by barbed wire, we inquired about it.

"Ah," Issa Awad replied, "that is the Embassy of the Soviet Union. Almost all Syrians hate it. Not one Syrian citizen, we are proud to say, works in that embassy. We wish the West, especially the United States, was our ally."

"Not one Syrian employee?"

"Not a single Syrian. You see," he added, "the Soviets are cold, unfriendly, and atheists. They do not worship or even recognize God. Their official government position is completely antagonistic to Islam and Christianity! We will not go near them. But since the West will not sell arms to Syria, what can we do to protect ourselves from Israel?"

* * * * *

As we checked into a very beautiful Sheraton Hotel, we were amazed at the modern design and quality. The marble floors, portions covered with huge Oriental carpets, high ceilings, and exquisite shops that bordered the lobby were stunning and busy with visitors. We were told the Meridian Hotel was equally luxurious, just a mile further.

We were guided to the main, large upscale dining room of the lobby and instantly gazed upward at the dramatic draped cloth ceiling emulating the inside of a tent, in keeping with the region's history and culture.

After we checked in, Sheryl and I took a cab to the city's main marketplace, the Himadayeh Souk, adjacent to the grand, enormous Omayyed Mosque. In the eighth century, the mosque was built in the place of an ancient, first century Christian church, the Basilica of Saint John the Baptist. Out of respect, we were told, the Muslims created the elegant resting place of the head of John the Baptist, whom they consider a prophet as do Christians, within the sarcophagus (altar tomb). The tomb of Saladin, the first sultan of Egypt and Syria, stands in a small garden adjoining the north wall of the mosque.

Damascus Himadeydh Souk: Sheryl purchasing Syrian
dress

The mosque displays the most important examples of Christian art during the Iconoclastic Controversy. The mosaic tiles throughout the mosque and on the walking area in the very large public area next to the mosque are extremely beautiful and should continue to be preserved for posterity. The architecture, the workmanship and designs are among the very finest examples in the Middle East.

The souk, one of the largest in the world, was bustling with people. It is similar to today's retail malls and about twenty-five hundred feet long, with an open walkway covered by a round, cavernous roof, with two story shops on either side of the covered central mall or street way. Shops mostly adorned the ground floor and many were two stories high. There were no vacant stores we noticed. We were reminded we were shopping with the others just before Christmas.

As we walked through the souk, hawkers urged us into their stores at every stop.

"Come in. Join us for tea or coffee."

Or, "Please come in and see what we have for you."

Persistent, but polite, they were everywhere. And since it was just a week before Christmas, the souk had Christmas decorations everywhere. And anything one wanted to purchase, whether gold bracelets, clothing, shoes, silks, nuts, *ouds* (Eastern guitars), souvenirs, cultural antiques, decorative swords and mosaics, crafted brass, Santa Claus dolls, linens, brass and silver urns. I was fascinated and Sheryl and

I felt compelled to buy presents for family back home.

We made our way through the crowds to the shop by the Roman columns of Jupiter, near the mosque owned by Ahmad Kahwaji, someone Sheryl knew from her earlier visit.

We were approached by an old man from whom Sheryl asked for directions. It turned out he worked for Ahmad. So he took us there, next to the Roman statue of Jupiter

It was fabulous and two stories. And Ahmad was most gracious.

"Sandy, we have only forty-five minutes to meet the ambassador! We have to hurry!"

"But there are so many wonderful things here! I could shop in this store for hours!" I replied, looking at all the overstuffed shelves and tables.

Both of us immediately began to pick our selections. Sheryl found a magnificent Syrian dress for her mother and an old Palestinian dress each unique in design, reflecting their slightly different cultures and a small wooden chest with mother of pearl inlay.

I bought so many things. I especially liked the mosaic antiques. There were mosaic chairs, tables, make-up boxes, and jewelry boxes I knew my family members back home would love. I even posed, at the urging of Ahmad, in a Syrian kiffeyeh, abeyeh and an Arabic headdress while holding an ancient sword theatrically across my chest.

The biggest problem was how in the world was I going to carry these things home in that tiny airplane?

Mosaic game table made circa1900, real inlaid mother of pearl, purchased at Damascus souk.

Mosaic game table opened up

Matching mosaic chair, one of two as a set with the table

Mosaic lap desk

Damascus, Syria: Children at play, selling Syrian bread

* * * * *

"Oops! Time to go."

We caught a taxi to the U.S. Embassy where we found out the meeting would instead be held at the residence of the ambassador. So, the two of us bundled our shopping bags filled with "wonders of the orient" for family members and rushed in a new taxi to his residence. We hurried in, being a few minutes late (so embarrassing!), and followed our staff guide to a lovely, airy sunroom in the ambassador's home. Hisham and Joe were already seated and exchanging pleasantries with Ambassador Seelye and his assistant, Mr. Walker.

110

Sheryl remembers him as tall and handsome. The sunroom was enclosed by large, clear windows overlooking a picturesque garden of fruit trees, including oranges, grapefruits, and pomegranates, all bearing colorful fruit.

We had a pleasant, detailed, yet, quite informative discussion, mostly listening to Ambassador Seelye. He certainly had a firm grasp of the situation throughout the Middle East. We asked if Syria would be willing to sign a regional peace treaty with Israel. "Only if the Golan, East Jerusalem and the West Bank were returned."

He squarely put the blame of the current Lebanese civil war on the heads of Lebanon's powerful Maronite families, especially the Chamoun and Gemayel families. He also repeated the advice of Prince Turki and King Khalid urging us to convince President Assad to be more concerned with accurate information dissemination and public relations, especially with the Western powers. We spent more than two hours with Ambassador Seelye.

"What do the locals say about the Camp David agreement, Mr. Seelye?" I asked.

He first reminded us that Secretary of State Cyrus Vance and Senator Byrd of West Virginia had recently visited Damascus prior to the signing of the Camp David Accords seeking the views of President Assad regarding the then ongoing global peace conference in Geneva.

Ambassador Seelye informed us that President Assad had met with President Carter in Geneva prior to the signing of the Accords. President Carter and Secretary Vance then wanted President Assad's position on an overall, regional peace agreement with Israel. I understand President Assad told them he was ready and willing to make peace with Israel in the context of a regional peace agreement with all parties including the Soviet Union, Palestinians, Jordan and Lebanon. Looking at each of us for emphasis, Ambassador Seelye reminded us that all the parties were indeed in Geneva seeking a regional peace agreement, but Israel and Egypt left Geneva.

Since the signing of the Accords between Israel and Egypt, he and the rest of the Arab World felt that they, King Hussein and President Assad were insulted and blindsided by the United States and Israel.

"How did President Carter and President Assad get along during their meeting," Joe asked. "And what did President Carter ask of President Assad?"

After a moment of thought, Ambassador Seelye replied, "President Carter, I know, is determined to find a way toward a regional peace. We know that. He asked Assad, 'Where do we go from here? How do we bring peace to the region and not just Israel and Egypt?'

"President Carter and Secretary Vance are hopeful," he continued, "and believe other Arab countries will join Egypt in signing a peace accord with Israel."

We told him our findings concluded that they would agree to a regional peace agreement with Israel only if Israel agreed to accept a Palestinian state in the West Bank and Gaza, restoration of their human rights, return of the Golan, Gaza, and East Jerusalem, all of which were not agreed to in the signed Camp David Peace Accords.

After very informative discussions, we told him we were scheduled to meet with President Assad the next day and was there anything we could do to convey any American wishes or requests of President Assad. But, reluctantly, we had to excuse ourselves due to an appointment with His Majesty Abdul Halim Khaddom, Syria's Minister of Foreign Affairs scheduled for 7:15 p.m. and it was now nearly seven o'clock.

* * * * *

As we arrived at the Ministry, we were able to view the reception room, filled with hand-carved furniture, damask, silk covered chairs inlayed with mother of pearl. The floors were covered with Oriental rugs similar to the airport reception room.

Here's what the minister told us:

"We have had multinational joint action for fulfillment of justice and peace in the region that requires the withdrawal of Israel, and restoration of Palestinian rights based on U.N. Resolutions 242 and 338.

"In 1974, just four years ago, 105 nations voted for Palestinian rights. We witnessed a greater understanding for the lack of their human rights as a people under the Israeli, rights Allah has given all of mankind. The Third World understood their terrible, imprisoned lives. Apparently, the United States does not care about the human rights of anyone when Israel is the occupier.

"But the West's understanding only came by realization of the importance of the area as it relates only to oil, not the human rights of the people. This realization led the West to minimize Arab demands. So, we find 105 nations understanding the conditions on one side and the U.S. on the other side with Israel. What is it that we did to cause the U.S. to ignore the human rights of the Palestinians? Was it simply because they were in the way of the Zionists and the Americans?

"As a result of Sadat's visit to Jerusalem and neutralizing the most populated Arab nation, Egypt, our influence has diminished. Sadat's visit is without precedence in history. We have to divide events before and after his visit to Jerusalem.

"Our relationship with the West has colonial roots. Sadat's visit was welcomed by the West because it supports Israel's neocolonialism. The media fooled Sadat. He thought he was now a different human being, a much elevated faux statesman. He believed his visit improved his political standing in Egypt, which, of course, it did not. As you know, he was not elected president. He was appointed by the powers of Nasser.

"How, we ask, can the U.S. say it believes in human rights and democracy and wants Sadat to be president of Egypt? By his visit, the region's balance changed dramatically. Now, a major member of the Arab world is aligned with the enemy."

* * * * *

As Minister Khaddom described the thinking and the conditions from the Syrian and Arab perspective, we listened intently and took copious notes, verbatim, as much as possible. We were now receiving more insight and details we could deliver to Secretary Vance and

114

President Carter. Clearly, the Arab world leaders looked on Sadat and his actions as betrayal to heighten his own personal esteem in the West, and for his own political standing in Egypt.

"And what did Sadat receive for all he gave? The Sinai Desert. What is that good for? It's barren and cannot support many people. He got nothing for the Palestinian people, and he did not advance the cause for peace in the region.

"Now, we are convinced that with the support of the U.S., Pax Israel will be imposed on the Arabs for at least thirty, maybe forty years. By then, the Arab oil reserves will be diminished.

"Secretary Vance asked us during his visit several weeks ago if we wanted peace. We said yes, emphatically. But we also told him that the road Sadat and Israel are traveling won't lead to peace. Sadat's visit is the same as when Rudolph Hess went to England. The only difference is that Hess was imprisoned in England."

Once again we were impressed with the knowledge of events outside the Middle East by the ministers and heads of state we met with.

The minister continued, "We told Secretary Vance the importance of understanding the difficulties imposed on Syria and other Arab states because of the enormous influx of refugees from Palestine because of Israel's actions.

"Israel now has taken all of Palestine. It has 'ethnically cleansed,' as you call it, Palestine of more than 8,000 villages, and continues to absorb more land. They claim it is for their security, but we know it is to expand Israel as much as possible, using their Bible to suit political desires of the hard line Zionists and their extremist Likud Party."

"It had now been thirty years since the U.N. and the U.S. created the State of Israel, and no Arab leader has had the power to stop Israel's colonial expansion. Israel says they only want secure borders. Which borders? we ask. They keep changing their borders, expanding all the time; some of Syria, some of Egypt, some of Lebanon now all of Palestine East Jerusalem and some of Jordan. What if Canada took some of your northern states like Montana and the Dakotas then said they want secure borders but included those states? How would Americans react? Please tell us.

"During World War II, the U.S. didn't sign a separate treaty with Hitler. It had to include all the nations of Europe. Why should this be different?

"We don't seek to kill the Jewish people, as we know many Israelis are good people, or 'drive Israel into the sea' as your media and pandering politicians claim. That is propaganda from the Israelis, not our views. We believe only a region peace agreement will bring peace to the Middle East, a regional peace with honor and justice. Sadat could only deal with the Sinai. Where is the U.S. support for those pitiful people in Palestinian refugee camps? Who mandated Sadat to sign for Jordan, Syria, Lebanon, and the rest of the Arab world?" the minister asked.

"In U.N. Resolution 338, third paragraph, it states 'there should be a conference under U.N. auspices with all parties participating,' and U.N. Resolution 242 requires the return to pre-1967 borders.

"Who mandates Carter and Sadat to go against international

legitimacy? As strong as the U.S. is, they could not defeat the Vietnamese. Crusaders from Europe stayed here for more than 130 years, and now only castles remain for American tourists to visit. No nation can swallow another. Camp David is a warrior against peace."

His Excellency Minister of Foreign Affairs Abdul Halim Khaddom impressed us with his global knowledge, his candor, and his courage. As Americans, albeit of Arabic heritage, we keenly sought his nuances and Syria's perspective, which are totally absent in debates in Washington or on U.S. TV and printed media coverage. Our eyes must have reflected our American viewpoint, especially after thirty years of pro-Israel American media and political propaganda.

* * * * *

After our tea and biscuits were refreshed, he continued by adding, "We are not pessimistic. We have faced these things before. We, as an ancient people, have a history of foreign occupation and colonialism, beginning with the Egyptians whose leader was toppled when the Egyptians signed an alliance with the Crusaders and recognized Jerusalem as part of the Crusader state. So too, Sadat has signed an alliance with the Zionists. So, we see history repeat itself as an idea, not as individuals. After the Egyptians signed with the Crusaders, Saladin went to Egypt and toppled their ruler. It is ironic that during the 200-year Crusade occupation, the Arabs were the ones who protected the Jews from the Western Christian invaders. After the Crusaders left Palestine, it was Saladin, a Syrian, who invited them back. And today, Westerners, now Zionist Jews, have come here, taken our lands, our homes, and our freedom. First it was the Greeks, the Romans, the Crusaders, or as we describe that era, the "Western invasion," and now Israel's Zionists. It may take a great deal of time, but we believe the next thirty to fifty years will be brutal under the U.S. financed Israelis. History continues to repeat itself. So, we have learned to accept our fate and look to the long term. It's very much an Eastern concept.

"In the October 1973 war, Syria's army was one and one-half the size of the Egyptian army. Syria is currently only nine million people, but we have one million under arms. It was only after the U.S. sent all its arms in Europe from NATO that Israel was able in the last days to win the war.

"Where are Carter's Arabs?" he asked rhetorically.

"At the conference in Baghdad, all the Arabs were unanimous in support of the Confrontation States. The Arab world is very big with lots of resources. And even though Camp David has now created a new reality, where are the friends of the U.S.? The Shah of Iran who cannot last long? The South Vietnamese?

"The U.S. is short-sighted. We want peace, but peace with honor, a peace that will not shame us before our children; a peace that will endure.

"All the Palestinians desire, as your brilliant founder Thomas Jefferson believed, is their God-given human rights to live free of occupation by the Israelis, and to live in peace. And really, that's all we want too.

"We know Israel exists. But which Israel? It must be the Israel that does not include its illegally taken lands in 1967 including Syria's Golan, the West Bank, East Jerusalem, and Gaza.

"It seems that while the U.S. says they respect their own public opinion, they do not allow Arab leaders to respect their own public opinion. The U.S. President must consult with Congress, but Sadat did not consult with his own people before going to Jerusalem. Sadat went there to get the Sinai back and to elevate his own esteem and political position. But he made a huge mistake. It accomplished neither except popularity in the Western media and a portion of the U.S. government's treasury. Our main task now is to re-establish equilibrium. Before this equilibrium in the region occurs, any talks will not bring peace. There must be a balanced focus.

"As long as Begin has all the guns, tanks, jet fighters, and other advanced American arms, there will be no balance, and therefore, no point in talks. Peace cannot come when one side is far too strong militarily.

"When the entire Arab world, including Egypt, was united, we had the support of international opinion. Yet, Begin stated that Palestine, including the West Bank, is to be part of Israel. Now that Israel is so strong, thanks to the U.S., why should he give anything to Sadat? They both ignore the needs and inherent rights of the Palestinians."

* * * * *

We listened carefully to what Minister Khaddom was saying,

119

taking verbatim notes that appear here. Seeking to fully understand Syria's perspective, Joe asked, "How then do you see peace between the Arabs and Israel?"

His reply was succinct and clean. The message we would also write verbatim and take to Secretary Vance:

"First, Israel must vacate and return all territories taken in 1967. Second, Palestine must be recognized as a state as stated in U.N. resolutions. Third, any settlement must be within the framework of the U.N. resolutions. There must be a peace accord of all the nations in this region, including Israel. Peace and security with honor, a state and freedom of human rights for the Palestinian people. And they must be compensated for the homes and farms taken from them.

"How can anyone, especially the Americans, not see these conditions as just? And the Israelis … how can a people so abused, who suffered so much themselves, not want to allow freedom, God-given human rights, for the Palestinians? We don't understand.

"Our view is that public opinion in the U.S. must and will change. But it will be a slow process. Attempts at distortion of the views of Americans toward the Arab World will continue as long as the U.S. media is controlled by Zionists.

"We will continue to seek peace. However, peace we seek in the full sense of the word, peace that is not subject to Israel's will. Peace is obtained throughout history as the result of many sacrifices of humanity. The illusions Israel is trying to impose are false. One of the illusions they seek to impose is something called guaranteed 'secure borders,'" Minister Khaddom stated with a sardonic smile of doubt.

"If the world adopts this as a principle, it will have to be adopted throughout the world, which means each nation in the Western Hemisphere, north to south, will have the right to claim territory from its neighboring countries under the pretext of assuming secure borders. And soon, all of Europe, Asia, and Africa will have to do the same. It is insanity. But Israel's ridiculous and impossible declaration is supported by the U.S. And, it makes no sense.

"Another thing Israel is trying to impose on the Arabs: Very often, President Carter speaks of human rights and one of the fundamental rights is the right to an education. And we believe he is sincere. But when it comes to the Palestinian people, he seems to us to be alone since the U.S. Congress appears opposed to helping the Palestinians obtain their own state and their human rights if it means Israel yielding any land. But there are other issues. As I said to Senator Byrd only a few days ago, here in Syria we teach our students the history of Syria and the Arab World in all aspects, all of its parts, whether we like them or not. We do the same with regard to the history of the U.S, France, and all of Europe.

"Now, Israel wants to reach a peace under which conditions are imposed on our education. For example, under Israel's conditions, we would not be able to teach our students of the Zionist movement as we see it; only from Israel's perspective which, of course, is completely biased. How can we say this is compatible with human rights? And how can we accept this as a requirement of peace? That is another reason why we say Israel is trying to impose capitulation on the Arabs. In truth, Israel does not want a true peace.

"And, concerning Lebanon, another hot spot, we have exerted continuous efforts at great expense and young Syrian soldiers in order to save Lebanon from blood baths. Israel promoted internecine war by supporting one Lebanese militia against the other. We have made big sacrifices in order to save Lebanese citizens. We view the citizens of Lebanon as part of our people and our own nation. We feel their pain and the calamity that befalls them as though they are Syrian citizens.

"We went into Lebanon in order to help all Lebanese and to prevent massacres there. And we have been successful. Yet, Israel controls Lebanon, occupies southern Lebanon and is deeply involved in Lebanon's civil war. The problem is there are certain powerful groups there who want us to be in the service of their narrow interests instead of being in the service of all Lebanese. This is the same internal conflict we ourselves face from time to time. We are sorry to see Israel has succeeded in involving itself into certain Lebanese political disputes in Lebanon. But we must endeavor to seek humanitarian and patriotic objectives. These same Lebanese elements that have joined with Israel have played a bad role in recent events."

His last comment was consistent with U.S. Ambassador Talcott Seelye's appraisal that the Gemayel and Chamoun families and their militias have conspired with Israel's military forces to rid Lebanon of the PLO and as many Palestinian refugees as possible.

Following our very candid and informative meeting, we enjoyed a wonderfully abundant lunch, which consisted of a grand *mezza* fit for a king! Included were a variety of Syrian dishes familiar to all of us: hummus, tabouli, kibbee, rice with noodles and pine nuts, and many unexpected dishes like oysters on the half shell, calamari, fishes, and other eastern Mediterranean delights. Our gathering with several ministers and officials provided us a genial atmosphere to exchange ideas, suggestions, and press our own welcomed views to improve

Syrian-American relations and the search for peace throughout the region.

Still, it was made clear to us that Syria would not consider a treaty of peace with Israel that did not include Israel's return to its 1967 borders, including the return of Syria's Golan, the West Bank, the establishment of human rights, and a state for the Palestinians, East Jerusalem and Gaza. There was little apparent difference within the Arab world. All told us the very same positions as if one nation, not several. It brought to mind the similarity of Native American tribes (like the Sioux, Apache, Navajo, et al.) seeing themselves as tribes of one nation, all seeking to protect their lands as one against the European conquest. *Now, I thought, aren't we supposed to be more enlightened, wiser and more civilized than we were 500 years ago?*

"The choice is America and Israel's," we heard several times. "There must be a balance of power in the Middle East before a true peace can reign over our region. Otherwise, whatever takes place will be imposed and unacceptable."

We felt privileged to be among these candid, informal discussions, and felt that we had received clear messages, definitive and comprehensive views of Syria's government, which our government representatives had been unable to receive in recent months even though we had not yet met with President Hafez Al Assad. Our appointment with him was set for the next day.

For me, spending these two days in the birthplace of my mother, her family, and my maternal ancestors, was a thrill I'll never forget. I was able to meet with my cousins, especially Maha Zein, a raven-haired, ebullient, fifteen-year-old beauty in my mother's father's family, and my grandfather's brother, then in his nineties, who looked just like my grandfather. He and I were overjoyed as we sat on his family couch, hugged, cried with joy, and spoke of his family now in America and Brazil. Maha and I tried to converse although neither of us spoke each other's language. But we had a great time laughing, using hand signals, and simply relishing this reunion. My mother often spoke of our two families in Damascus, the Al Zein (my maternal grandfather's family), and the Thomé (my paternal grandmother's) family, now mainly in Brazil, most of whom fled Syria in 1905 during the Ottoman conscription of Christian men into the Muslim armies. Note: Until the 1950s, there was a U.S. quota of two percent (2%) of the existing population, which meant to keep the U.S. predominantly northern European (English, French, German, Dutch, and Scot). As a result, most emigrants from Syria and other Mediterranean countries, including its then province of Lebanon, settled in Canada, Central and South America, and the Caribbean, all searching for freedom and opportunity. Some did stay in Syria for personal and family reasons, but as a result, by 1978, there were an estimated three to four million Americans of Syrian/Lebanese Christians in the U.S. as compared to about forty million in Latin America, nearly eight million in Brazil alone, and millions more in Chile, Argentina and other nations there. I felt a visceral appreciation for my family members and my heritage. Damascus truly is the "Jewel of the Middle East" with a long and complex history, of free enterprise, an abundance of private enterprises, small and large. The Christian community thrived under the secular government of Assad, an Alawite Shiia Muslim and the Ba'ath Party in a nation predominantly Sunni Muslim.

Maha Al Zein, Damascus, Syria, cousin of the author,
December 22, 1978

Maha Al Zein

It was so exciting to see the ancient ruins, historical city housing over several hundreds of years old, the enormous, hyperactive souk that was nearly three thousand years old, more than half a mile long, with more than five hundred shops of all kinds, the mosques, and, as we walked where St. Paul walked on "The Street Called Straight," I even felt a bond with my religious heritage.

We returned to the hotel for the night. The next morning we left our baggage at the hotel in Damascus and flew to Beirut for meetings with President Elias Sarkis of Lebanon ministers and other high officials and, homeland of my father and my paternal ancestors.

Throughout the short, twelve minute flight, we saw snow-capped Mount Hermon to the southwest, the snow covered Golan on the left and, to the right, we gazed on the seven thousand feet high mountains of Mount Lebanon where my father's birthplace village, Douma, was nestled in a valley three thousand, five hundred feet above sea level. All of Mount Lebanon was snow-covered, yielding a magnificent sight for us, especially as the sun reflected off the snow and the Mediterranean Sea.

It was an emotional moment for me that I will not forget. I felt a charge of electricity in my body as I looked down on Douma, where, legend tells me, my family ancestors, six Chalhoub brothers and their families, settled in 350 B.C.E. after leaving the Golan. At that time, the mountains around Douma were covered by stately, ancient cedars, some twenty-five years before Alexander the Great's Greek armies invaded the coastal city-states of Byblos, Sidon, and Tyre before conquering the southern region, including Palestine and Egypt.

Too quickly, it seemed, we touched down on the tarmac of the airport just south of the city of Beirut, "Paris of the Middle East," and where, we were told several times, we would "dine on the favorite foods of all the Middle East."

But Lebanon was in the middle of a heated civil war between the Maronite Christian militias, their allies, Israel's military and on the other side, the Muslims and PLO forces. The PLO was based in West Beirut and the Israelis were very much in the picture, seeking to destroy the PLO. So, my sublime fantasies were quickly replaced with the war zone realities and damage surrounding us. There were armed military all around the airport although the airport was nearly empty.

We were met with a car and driver and driven to the Presidential Palace in Baabda, in the hills east of and adjacent to Beirut, passing many checkpoints of the various combatants. We did not know whose militia was controlling the checkpoints. They looked the same to me, with sandbags piled high manned by lots of heavily armed men in uniforms, assault rifles at the ready. Few of the buildings in the city were free of battle scars, whether an arc of bullet holes sprayed by automatic rifles, some with enormous holes, perhaps eight to ten feet across from rockets, and evidence of hand-to-hand combat. There were other major noticeable and emotionally devastating symbols of change we saw as we drove on the seafront Corniche, which normally provided magnificent views of the cerulean blue water of the Mediterranean Sea. Instead, we drove past an enormously long unbroken line of makeshift shops made of scrap pieces of wood, and sheet metal roofs. These, we were told, were the replacement shops relocated from the city's historic souk where too much fighting occurred.

As we watched sadly, seeing the impact the war was having on the people, we were brought face to face with the untenable situation of the sectarian politics of the region. The Palestinian refugees, driven out of Palestine by the Israelis, had significantly impacted on the politics of Lebanon, a nation of perhaps four million Lebanese at that time, which was not able to cope with the influx of a million destitute Muslim Palestinians and the armed PLO. Some Maronite Christian families and their militias, fearful of a Muslim takeover of Lebanon, surreptitiously found allegiance with the Israeli military and its government since their common adversary was the Palestinians and the PLO, which sought to return to Palestine, using Lebanon as their base of operations having been forced out of Jordan.

As we were driven to the Presidential Palace, we witnessed and passed many more armed checkpoints again and again filled with men holding assault rifles at the ready, surrounded by sandbags stacked up as high as eight feet.

Our meeting with President Sarkis was a mix of pride, sadness, and excitement, and one we found very informative. A gentle man, whose heart clearly was bleeding with distress, responded to the Camp David Accords by telling us, "If there is no agreement on a Palestinian state, a place the pitiful refugees can return to, a place where we can deport them to, then the Lebanon we know and love will be no more. There are so many refugees here, nearly twenty percent of our population, and their presence together with the constant Israeli threat of invasion makes Lebanon a battleground for others and their allies. There are no guns or bullets manufactured in Lebanon, he emphasized. Only those brought here by outsiders including the United States, Israel, Libya and still others. We are awash in guns, bullets, and rockets brought into Lebanon by these militias and outsiders. We are in the vortex of a proxy war."

We learned so much from President Sarkis, but the conversation was somewhat depressing because the ongoing fighting was out of the control of the central government. Rather, it was a proxy war between war lords, and other countries, all of which were arming their particular allies, all fighting in the streets of Beirut.

At one moment during our conversation, the President was interrupted by a staff member who whispered in his ear as we watched. After he left, the president told us anxiously, "You must return to a safe place by a different route than the one you took to come here. Heavy fighting at the Green Line in central Beirut between the Phalange, a Christian militia, and the PLO is occurring. Hundreds of young men are being killed there as we speak."

Our incredible meeting with President Sarkis lasted over two hours. We also met with several ministers, including the Minister of the Interior; a distant cousin of Sheryl's who graciously offered us lifetime visas to Lebanon. Being of Lebanese heritage, and proudly so, we relished his kind offer as we viscerally felt the pain of the Lebanese people, our "extended family." And, we eagerly looked forward to returning time and again in the future.

These are people whose country had thrived and survived in a long history of open borders, free enterprise, human rights, *laissez-faire*, a tiny, ineffective national army, virtually no Navy or Air Force, living in the center of battles between heavily armed Israel, the PLO, and Syria. The people simply trying to survive the best they could. Even as we visited during the street fighting, civilians inherently displayed their characteristic sense *joie d'vivre,* a lust for life, finding a way somehow to enjoy even the worst of days We witnessed street peddlers pushing their wagons loaded with imported goods ranging from whiskey to shoes to foods, never giving in to the politics and the war.

After all of our meetings that day, we returned to the airport by another route to fly back to Damascus for our scheduled meeting with President Hafez Al Assad.

Chapter 11
Syria II

Promptly at 11:00 a.m. on Thursday, December 21, 1978, we arrived at our meeting in Damascus with President Hafez Al Assad, considered in the U.S. as an ally and client state of the Soviet Union and therefore an enemy of the U.S. during the Cold War, as well as an Arab Confrontation State, and an adversary of Israel; therefore, an enemy of the U.S.

Yet, we, as Arab-Americans, were warmly greeted by the soft-spoken, smiling president as we entered his comfortable meeting room of damask-covered couches, chairs, and small mosaic tables. We took our seats on a magnificent sizeable couch covered in silk damask with a carved wood frame. I selected the end of the couch, near where Assad was seated on a separate matching ornate chair. I noted with interest that throughout our meeting both his feet were flat on the floor next to each other. He never crossed his legs showing the bottoms of his shoes. Neither did we. I wanted to hear his words as clearly as possible, seeking, as in every meeting, to record verbatim all that he told us. And after asking for his approval, Sheryl and I took a few prized photographs of the president.

Although a translator sat next to the president, as it turned out, President Assad understood much of our English. At one point, after about an hour of conversation, to make sure I understood him exactly, I asked him if it was true what I thought I'd heard, looking to the translator for his response. To my surprise, President Assad looked at me and, with a very slight smile, replied to me in English!

We all suddenly realized that the past hour's conversation through the translator was not necessary, as President Assad understood our questions in English. Of course, we were willing to accept that as an assurance that what he thought he understood was exact. Yet we couldn't help but feel he was indeed a "sly fox," a political leader and a prominent and vital person in the realm of global and Middle Eastern politics.

Damascus: President Hafez Al Assad
during our three hour conference

Damascus: Meeting with President Assad: (L-R) Sandy
Simon, Hisham Sharabi, Sheryl Ameen, President Hafez
Al Assad, Joe Baroody, Assad's Chief of Staff

President Assad told us he was proud Arab-Americans were organizing themselves in order to make a difference in American politics "by making a beneficial contribution to your family, your ancestral motherland. We follow your activities as best we can and hope your visits will be more frequent. It's best that you and other Americans know things first hand. Facts from your own people here are more accurate than from your media.

"We believe that American foreign policy should be dictated only by American interests. But, sadly, they are convinced Israel should be the master of the Middle East."

"I inquired, "Why does the Syrian government align with the Soviet government, the Cold War adversary of the U.S.? Why don't you expand trade with and buy your arms from the U.S. or Western Europe?"

"Thank you," he said to me, "that is a fair question. In fact, we have sought to expand our trade with the West. We export many agricultural goods and manufactured equipment with the Soviet Union. But when we seek trade with the West, or to purchase goods, particularly arms with which to defend ourselves, we are completely rejected, especially by the U.S. When we sought arms from England or France, they told us the U.S. would frown on them selling arms to Syria, so, in the end, they offered just one tank and only for prepaid cash. We are convinced this is true because of the singular alliance of the West, especially the U.S. with Israel.

"So, we really have no choice but to seek trade and arms purchases from the Soviet Union. It is the same with Egypt, although it appears that will change for Egypt now that they have signed a treaty with Israel. So, Sadat's betrayal of the Arab world's efforts in seeking a balance with Israel will result in Egypt getting back only the Sinai, and improving its relations with the U.S. It is tragic Sadat and President Carter, whom I respect very much, did not obtain Israel's agreement to permit a Palestinian state, return the Golan, West Bank, and East Jerusalem. You see? We cannot have individual states sign with Israel any more than England, France, Belgium, or the Netherlands and the others negotiating separate peace treaties with Hitler. It never would have brought peace. That is why we seek a regional peace treaty with Israel.

"President Carter often speaks of human rights and America's efforts to insist on human rights across the world. But Palestinian rights seem to be the only human rights American policy excludes. Why is that?

"As I told Senator Byrd when he was here in Syria, we teach our students the history of Syria and the Arab world in all its aspects, good and bad, whether we like them or not. We do the same with regard to the history of France, England, and the U.S. But Israel wants us to reach peace by insisting we change our education system. For example, under Israel's imposition, we would not be permitted to teach our students about the Zionist movement as we see it. How can we teach our students a false history? How is this compatible with human rights and freedom to teach the truth? Israel demands we teach our children falsehoods of the Zionist takeover of Palestine. But we demand the freedom to teach the truth. Israel is trying to impose capitulation on the Arabs as a condition for peace."

"May I ask you a question?" Sheryl asked.

137

"Of course, Mrs. Ameen."

"Golda Meir is quoted as saying, 'We will have peace with the Arabs when they love their children more than they hate us.' What would you say to her?"

"Excellent question. I would tell Golda Meir that the Arabs love their children and the freedom of the Palestinian people far more than we hate anyone. We have lived among the Jews for centuries. Even during the Western Invasion which you call The Crusades. The Arabs and Muslims protected the Jewish people from annihilation by the Western Christians ... for two hundred years we protected them. And after the Westerners left, defeated by Saladin, we invited the Jewish people to return to Palestine! Even today, Jews and Christians in Syria are free. They are prosperous shopkeepers, doctors, lawyers and workers of all kinds. They are safe in Syria and are peace loving people. Syrians don't hate Jews. They are considered spiritual cousins as we all are sons of Abraham. The Koran follows the prophet Moses as do the Jews. And the Koran tells us our belief in Jesus as a prophet of God whom we, in Arabic call Allah. They are one and the same. We all worship the same living, loving God. It is true that for more than one thousand years Jews, Muslims and Christians lived in peace among themselves. Each had their own villages across Palestine, trading, visiting, children playing together. Of course, intermarriage rarely if ever occurred. But they had their freedom of worship, freedom of movement, and no army occupied their villages. Now, it is different under the Zionists whose only belief, whose goals are to establish a purely Jewish state in all of Palestine. They consider all of Palestine and perhaps all lands to the Euphrates as their ancestral land. That would include Lebanon and much of Syria in addition to Gaza, ancestral land of the Philistines. Even now, they have taken and occupied Syria's

Golan, a fertile land farmed by Syrians for thousands of years, long before Moses came out of Egypt. So, to Golda Meir, we do not hate Jews, but we will have peace when the Jews and the Zionists go back to worshipping Allah, God, instead of the worship of more and more land, the goal of taking other people's homes, farms, and their freedom.

"I would say that we will have peace when the United States considers Arabs as people of mankind. As Thomas Jefferson wisely believed, all of mankind has the right to pursue happiness, and are to be ruled only by God, and governed only by those to whom the people have given their consent. And the Palestinians certainly have not given the Zionists their consent. Yet, they have no freedom or the right to pursue happiness.

"It is not true that we hate Jews," he reiterated, "more than we love our children. Every child is loved by their families, even their extended families. All children are required to obtain an education, which is free to all people in Syria, Iraq, Lebanon, Jordan, and more. We have many universities where equal numbers of women and men attend. Every child in the secular states of Syria, Lebanon, Iraq, Jordan, and other Arab countries is loved by their families and by their government.

"She is totally, completely wrong. But she is a total Zionist, having left behind her Jewish tenets. That, Mrs. Ameen, is what I would say to Golda Meir.

"With regard to Lebanon," he added after a moment of thought, "we have spent treasures continuously in efforts to save Lebanese citizens. We have made great sacrifices on behalf of the Lebanese citizens to save them from a bloodbath. We view the citizens of Lebanon as part of our people and our nation. We feel the pain for any calamity that befalls them, as we do for Syrian citizens.

"We went into Lebanon in order to prevent massacres there. The problem is that certain groups in Lebanon want us to be in their narrow service, their narrow interests and objectives instead of in the service of all Lebanese.

"We can only carry out our mission in Lebanon with honor. We refuse to have it recorded in history that we were not honest to our patriotic national and humanitarian approach in Lebanon.

"We are sorry to say that Israel has succeeded in allying with certain Lebanese. The Israelis provide the militia with guns, rockets, and aerial support. Why? Why are they allowed to do this in Lebanon?

"In contrast, we went into Lebanon in response to the request from the Lebanese government and calls of distress from many families there. At this present time, we have sent troops and placed them under the authority of the Lebanese government. If you took a poll in Lebanon, you would find a great majority of Lebanese are against our withdrawal. And it is for the sake of the majority that we accept their wishes and will continue to make costly sacrifices on their behalf. Even though we entered Lebanon at the request of the elected authority, the West and its pro-Israel media took a strong stand against us. Their stance had material consequences, which meant losses to Syria. They did not call for the removal of Israeli forces. However, we did not hesitate to carry out our duty. So, by staying, Syria made enormous sacrifices of our young men and women, our economic resources, and we continue as long as Israel occupies the south of Lebanon. We believe a balance of power there is the only way to bring about peace in Lebanon," Assad said.

"To give you a comparison of our sacrifices, the U.N. has 6,000 international troops in Lebanon with very light equipment, none in northern Israel to separate Lebanese from Israeli forces. In contrast, we had to send 40,000 troops with full equipment. Syria, almost alone, bears the cost of maintaining this force. Of course, we have mostly symbolic, and some financial, support from others in the Arab world. Syria has no selfish interests in remaining there. And if the Lebanese government would ask us to leave, we would do so immediately. Has Israel agreed to do the same?

"During the past four years of war in Lebanon, most of the world has offered advice and good words, but only Syria has done something toward stopping the war and helping the Lebanese citizens."

At this moment, Hisham offered words of appreciation from the Arab-American community, mostly Lebanese/Syrian-Americans.

In response, President Assad expressed this thanks for the opportunity to meet with us. He commented, "We highly appreciate your mission and the role you are playing. No one should underestimate the importance of your mission. It is an honor for us to see that you have such noble views and efforts that are motivating you. In light of this, we are certain peace and the future is in our favor. Your children should come and visit. If anything is required of us, we will contribute and cooperate. It is important to maintain contact between you and the Motherland."

We asked him if he had a message for President Carter.

"Tell him that like him, we stand for human rights. After meeting President Carter in Geneva, I had very good impressions of Carter, the man. I maintain that position although we differ politically on the question of peace. The path the U.S. is following will not lead to peace. I believe President Carter is seeking peace among all nations of the Middle East. But, America has made Israel very powerful; it cannot influence the neo-colonialists of Israel. What this agreement between Israel and Egypt is doing is planting the seeds of more conflict, perhaps a new war. Perhaps a different kind of war. I say that because we do not have the military power the U.S. has given Israel, but the feelings of some angry young Arab men are hardening toward Israel and the United States, I am sad to say. I am sad because almost all Syrians love, admire and respect the United States … except when it comes to the support of Israel's treatment of Palestinians, Arabs and Muslims.

"All of these things I tell you now, I told to Secretary of State Vance and Senator Byrd. Zionism, I told them, was the obstacle to peace.

"America must recognize there is a distinct difference between U.S. and Zionist interests. They are not at the same. Rather, actually, they conflict with each other."

We again came forward with comments and questions during this opportunity for discussion and enjoyed a give and take conversation during the next hour.

I urged that Syria improve its informational services to the American people to improve Syria's reputation in the U.S. I urged Assad to visit the U.S. himself, meet with political and business leaders and speak to the American people on television.

Sheryl followed up with a request that President Assad must visit not only Washington, but tour and speak in other major cities so that the American public could see him and hear him first hand, not through the filter of the pro-Israel media, which already holds a bias against Syria and the Arab world.

Joe Baroody concluded our opportunity to comment by again thanking President Assad for his role in Lebanon with which we all agreed.

Our rich and informative meeting with President Assad lasted one hour and forty minutes.

We then embraced the President customarily, one at a time. Photos with him and each of us separately and as a group were taken, after which we all left for a lunch at the Ministry of Presidential Affairs in our honor, given by President Assad.

But en route, we were guided to the offices of Abdul Karim Aadi, Minister of State for Foreign Affairs.

Our meeting with him went as follows:

"I heard of your mission and activities only a short while ago. Our Arab voice is not able to effect political dialogue, but working together, we should address American public opinion. Our policy is to develop relations with the Arab-American communities in Latin America because there is no animosity toward the Arab world there. Latin America is filled with successful businesses owned by Syrian Americans. We are told there are tens of millions in Latin America. We have only just begun to get the support of the American public opinion, and you are our main access. We must pool our potential. There are shortcomings, but the Arab League is trying, although ineffective in this respect. The Arab League represents all its members, but cannot effectively represent Syria's point of view. We gave the Arab League our proposals for exchanges of visits of U.S. Congressmen, journalists, student cultural exchanges, and many more possibilities. We need your recommendations on how to provide impetus."

We offered suggestions one after the other of actions the Syrians could take, including, especially, student exchange programs, and a speaking tour of the U.S. and with lobbyists in Washington.

Damascus: Mezza hosted by President Assad.
Sheryl on left, Sandy with Syrian government dignitaries

* * * * *

After our meeting of about one hour, we went to lunch at a grand, popular restaurant in the center of Damascus. As we drove by parks and tree-lined neighborhoods, we even spotted a tall statue of Saladin, conqueror over the Western invaders a thousand years ago. We were greeted by our host, General Zouhair Ghazal, Secretary General for Presidential Affairs. We were all seated at a long table with each of the four of us scattered among the Syrian dignitaries. The Syrian officials were dressed in Western clothing, including suits and ties, although a few did wear their dishdashes and kiffeyehs. The efficient and pleasant waiters, all young men, were at our elbows at the slightest signal serving the customary appetizers of baba ghanoush, hummus, raw kibbee, kibbee neyeh, zeytoon (olives), oysters, lobster, fishes of all kinds, and Syrian bread which most used to wrap the food, using forks and knives only when necessary. Juices, tea, and water were also served. We also feasted on chicken, rice, and laban yogurt, and a beef roll with ham and cheese. Then, dessert and fruit. What an incredible *mezza*. We all felt stuffed when we finished the most wonderful feast, which, we all agreed, we had ever had the pleasure of enjoying. Damascus had a reputation for its history, cuisine, art, public parks, five star hotels, and especially, a 3,000-year-old souk, marketplace, where whatever you sought or were induced to purchase was available. Even if the merchant didn't have your selection, he would obtain it for you in minutes even if he had to retrieve it from his own living room. (Likely to the distress of his wife.) That is exactly how I was able to purchase two antique inlaid mosaic chairs to match the amazing, antique mosaic folding table that converts to backgammon, chess, or game table that I cherish to this day. (See photos.)

During our sumptuous meal we enjoyed and a variety of discussions on all topics. After, we stood and began the customary thirty minutes or more of thanks, embraces, comments, expressions of gratitude and pleasure together after which the government-sent limousine arrived and ingested the four of us. In the limo, we joyfully recaptured our almost unbelievably candid and lengthy discussions with several prominent and influential ministers crowned by our one hour-45 minute meeting with President Hafez Al Assad as we were whisked eastward from the center of the city and government offices to the airport, some twenty miles away.

Impressed as we were with the sincerity of the officials, we couldn't help but wonder aloud some of our thoughts.

Joe started by saying, "They all remind me of our friends in America. I mean virtually all Syrian/Lebanese Americans including each of us have many Jewish friends and business associates whom we respect completely. There is no prejudice within the Syrian/Lebanese American community that I know of."

"I agree, Joe," I added. "At home, I remember my parents attending numerous Bar Mitzvahs and Bat Mitzvahs at the invitation of their friends and my father's business colleagues. I don't get the problem here. Everybody told us they want peace. And if you believe the U.S. media and our politicians, so do the Israelis."

"I am not convinced the Israelis want peace," declared Hisham. "Many in the Muslim world believe they want to rule the Middle East with the United States as their ally and supplier. And they believe many in Washington want them to do so, and that means the young radicals will look on Israel and America as one entity: the enemy to be destroyed. I am fearful this could explode any time with painful results for Americans.

"And don't forget, there are millions of active of Christian Zionists in America, mostly fundamentalists who believe the establishment of Israel is God's will, " I added.

I laughed, "Religions sure have a way of separating people! As an Episcopalian, I am able to get along with all religions."

Still, we were baffled as to why more peaceful efforts between the parties, like cultural and student exchanges, weren't being tried.

I asked, "Israel has a terrific symphony orchestra, they all play soccer, and on and on. Maybe a people to people conference without governments involved would be helpful? What do you think, Hisham?"

"Theoretically it's a good idea. So is economic and business trade. I think the reason Egypt and Israel are signing their agreement is because the U.S. is paying them off. As they say, politics follows economics and trade."

As we were whisked eastward from the center of the city and government offices to the airport, Sheryl exclaimed, "Look, Sandy, there is the Soviet embassy. You can tell because it is so huge, and just a plain design of untreated concrete."

"Wow," I replied. "And see the guard towers and wire-topped outer walls. Weren't we told that in the humungous building complex not one Syrian national works there? I think that is quite a bold statement, don't you?

"I'm sad to leave Damascus, Sheryl. The hotel was so "Arabic" in design, the officials and other people so energetic, free and kind to us. And I was able to meet my family members here, on my mother's father's side, the Al Zein and Thomé families. You should meet my beautiful teenage cousin, Maha. She is terrific!"

"And the souk!" Sheryl laughed. "I'm going to miss the souk. It's huge with so many shops! And all those tourists from every country in the world, it seemed. From Morocco, Europe, South Americans, Iran, the Gulf States, Saudi Arabia … in their dress style … even in December!"

"Of course, Iran is not part of the Arab world, but Iranians do come here for the ease of shopping and to shop for Western products nonetheless."

* * * * *

We were driven directly to our Lear jet parked on the tarmac near the main terminal, watched over by our two pilots and a government guard.

"Well, Sheryl, here we go to our final meeting in Beirut."

"We didn't really know for certain if our hoped for meeting with Chairman Arafat will actually take place. Hisham said we won't be able to confirm until we are in Beirut. He told me Arafat wasn't even in Lebanon today, so we'll have to see when we get there."

"Yes, I heard Hisham say he may be in Tunisia."

Settled in the small jet with Hisham and Joe in the front seats (of course), and Sheryl and I relegated to the rear seats (of course), we left the ground on takeoff around five o'clock p.m.

Once again, during our surprisingly short flight of twelve minutes (the Middle East issues, which seem to consume the foreign policy of the U.S., seemed so obvious to solve to us.

I commented, "Most of the people on both sides want peace. They are willing to give because they all know they're better off with peace. And, I think, both sides know pretty much what the maps will look like in the end, but no side will give a little first. I think only the U.S. can make it happen. Maybe secret direct negotiations in a neutral location without the press would bring better results?" I asked.

Sheryl replied, "You know, Sandy, that makes good sense, I mean, this is all about politics. And politicians cannot negotiate freely with the press and the world watching. The political opposition always complains and attacks those negotiating.

"We and they know that ultimately Israelis, above all want virtual guarantees from the world that they are secure and will never be made to suffer as they have in Europe over the centuries."

"And, you know, Sheryl, I can't blame them. As a Christian, I'm ashamed of what Christians have done as they broke covenants with God in doing that to the Jews."

Hisham interjected, "Sandy, Sheryl, I agree with all you are saying. It is true that the Israelis feel a visceral fear of all non-Jews and believe they must find a way to guaranteed security. And, I believe they can have security, especially in America. I believe they are, but you and they must understand they are and for one hundred years been treating the Palestinian people the very same way they were treated. As a Palestinian, an Arab and a Muslim, I believe my people and the entire Arab World will agree to diplomatic and commercial relations, secure borders and the fulfillment of peace for everyone in the region. But the Israelis must stop taking our land, return to the pre-1967 borders and stop creating new borders by taking more and more Arab land then insisting those new borders must be secure. I mean: Which Israel is to be secure?"

As we flew the twelve minutes to Beirut we came to realize more than any other place on the globe, this troubled unstable spot is so tiny with so little distance, so few minutes' flight, between the capitals of the belligerent nations of Jordan, Israel, Syria, Lebanon, and even Iraq, not one of them feels safe from the other. So much distrust and fear pervades the entire region and somehow, we agreed, that must be changed into trust and willingness to live in peace together.

It was a profound feeling to suddenly become aware of the scale of the region whose strange, inexplicable national boundaries that were artificially imposed by the colonial powers of England and France after World War I and the defeat of the Ottoman Empire.

Lebanon is the smallest state by far, abutting Israel to the north, only 160 miles long, north to south, 40 miles wide, sea to Syria, along the east shoreline of the Mediterranean Sea. Palestine, now Israel, is nearly three times the size of Lebanon, depending on which Israel one considers. Jordan, with its bizarre arbitrary borders, is much larger, land-locked, poor, and mostly desert.

Syria, home (in 1978) to twelve million people and 24 million in 2013 at this writing, is a mix of commercial and banking centers, flat farmland that stretchers for miles and miles bordered by mountains in the north, west and along the south. The country, an ancient breadbasket and government center for 400 years under the Ottomans is a blend of prolific farm lands covered in wheat, pistachio, fruit and olive groves, mountains in the north, with lakes, vineyards and fruit orchards, and the several large, urban centers of Damascus, Aleppo, the nation's financial center, Homs, and Latakia, the major seaport on the Mediterranean, just north of Lebanon. If not for the region's instability, Syria could be a major tourist destination with its abundant ancient ruins of the Greek, Roman and Islamic periods.

"Look, Sandy, to the left are the Golan Heights completely covered in deep snow. Mount Hermon is snow covered as well."

We were seeing again those mountains we saw the day before, yet it was almost doubly exciting as we approached Beirut where we would conclude our extraordinary mission visits.

"And over here, Sheryl, on the right are the ranges of Mount Lebanon where the Christians have lived since Matthew, Peter, and Paul created the first Christian church in Antioch, Syria, which is now in Turkey. North Lebanon has been the safe haven for Christians since resisting the Islamic conversions in the 700s and 800s and where Jews and Muslims hid in caves, safe from the Crusaders. My father's family still lives down there," I said, pointing to where I thought nestled the scorpion-shaped village of Douma. "They tell me these mountains are over seven thousand feet above sea level, and because of the moisture from the sea, these mountains sometimes get more than forty-five feet of snow during the winter months."

"That's a lot of snow!" Sheryl laughed.

151

In only a minute or so, Sheryl pointed out the window. "There it is, Sandy. Beautiful Beirut. See the point into the sea? West Beirut is where the PLO is based and where most of the significant fighting is occurring." Then, she added, "I'm excited we may meet with Chairman Arafat tonight, but I'm a little sad because this might be our last meeting, and tomorrow we return to Amman, leave this plane, and begin our journey back home."

"Yeah, Sheryl, I'm sad too. I sure would like to visit my father's brother, Milhelm and his family, in Douma, about an hour's drive north of Beirut, while we are here, so close."

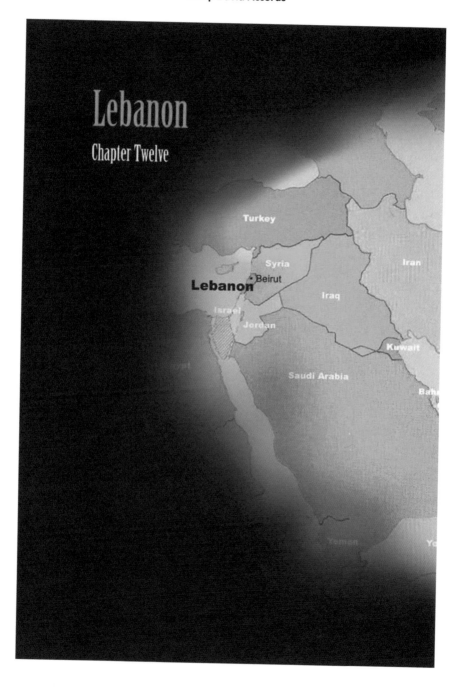

Lebanon

Chapter Twelve

Chapter 12
PLO & Arafat

In seconds, it seemed, we touched down in Beirut's airport, coming in from the west, having flown a wide arc as we crossed the mountains toward the sea, then banked to the left to land before the Lebanese mountains only a mile or two from the coast. It was getting dark when we landed. In Lebanon, we were not guests of the government; we were staying at Hisham's friend, Khalid's, sister's apartment near Hamrah Street, where the most fashionable shops are located. His sister was out of the city due to the fighting.

En route, we stopped in downtown West Beirut so Hisham could make personal contact with the PLO officials seeking to confirm a meeting that night with Chairman Arafat. While he was inside, we parked at a street intersection. There was rubble everywhere, damage from fighting shown on every building. It was starkly depressing and, I must say, a bit frightening to us who really had never been in the middle of an active war zone. There were sounds of automatic weapons being fired in volleys, and occasionally, a bomb, grenades or rocket shell exploding only a few streets away.

The dichotomy of warfare: Killing, wounding, and mayhem going on just a few blocks away while merchants and maintenance people were actually plastering over scarred stucco exteriors with their laborers mixing plaster in flat, large pans on the ground. Meanwhile, just a few feet away from us in the intersection surrounded by rubble, was a lonely standing water pipe topped by a hand-turned faucet being used by a tall, beautiful, fashionably dressed, long-haired woman in high heels who looked like she just left the runway of a fashion house in Paris. She was filling two bottles of water for her home. I stood by the taxi, amazed at her aplomb, the savoir faire of the Beiruti people to venture out, elegantly dressed, nails polished, in high heels "at the well" in the midst of a nearby civil war. She seemed indifferent and accepting of the street battles, shrugging it off perhaps as if to say, "Life must go on even if these over-testosteronized men must shoot at each other. Idiots!"

"How resilient are these people!" Sheryl said. "Either that, or how stupid!" But then, we're standing only feet away from the woman.

"So who's stupid? Her or us?" Sheryl's voice went up an octave as she exclaimed, watching the woman, "If my mother knew I was standing here in the middle of West Beirut now, with all the fighting she sees on television, she would have a heart attack!"

I laughed. "You are so right, Sheryl. How did we allow ourselves to come to the center of a civil war? I don't even have a BB gun!"

Beirut: Yassir Arafat with Hisham Sharabi

* * * * *

Hisham returned to us after about twenty minutes in the PLO offices as we stood unarmed, hopelessly vulnerable, but clearly not looking like militiamen or Palestinian fighters, so we were "off limits." What a sight. We were just a few blocks from the designated "green line" separating Maronite Christian militias from the Muslim Palestinians where, we were told later, more than 40,000 … forty thousand! One percent of the total population of Lebanon! Young men in a nation of just four million had been killed.

"Sheryl", I exclaimed. "That would be the same as 250,000 people killed in America! Think of that!"

"That is too horrible to think about, Sandy!"

After Hisham returned to the cab and instructed the driver where to deliver us, we were taken to Khalid's sister's condominium apartment where we were to wait for word from Arafat's offices. It was now after six p. m., getting dark, and we were at the total mercy of God. I silently prayed a lot.

"Are you okay, Sheryl?" I asked as we rode in the rear seat.

"Well, to be honest," she replied, "I'm pretty anxious about this. Hisham doesn't tell us anything, keeping all he knows to himself," she whispered. "You and I are completely in the dark, and it's so dark outside too," she nervously laughed. "I just pray the Lord is with us, Sandy. And I did call my cousin Salah who is the Minister of Interior and he told me the safest part of Beirut is the area around Arafat! So don't worry!

"It's not at all similar to our seven other stops. No government vehicles, no guards, no officials, and yet sounds of gunfire everywhere. This is the first time I feel a little nutty about being on this mission, I must admit," she added.

"I kind of feel the same way, Sheryl. While I really don't feel particularly safe, I'm not scared really, but I do feel a little naïve being in such a dangerous place. Let's not think about the fighting nearby or we'll fall apart! Somehow, I feel like it's going to be fine, and we'll be out of Beirut tomorrow."

We were driven through the labyrinth of winding, narrow streets of West Beirut, finally arriving in front of our "safe house," a mid-rise condominium of six stories, the same as most in the neighborhood. We went through the entry with our luggage, walked to the single elevator, taking it to the fifth floor and entered the lovely but sparsely furnished two-bedroom, two-bath apartment. We were originally told to wait in the sixth floor apartment, but that morning it had been hit by a rocket and was badly damaged and unsafe. There was an eight foot wide hole in its outer wall.

Most of the street fighting was taking place in West Beirut, where the PLO was based during the war, having fled from Jordan. The entire time there we listened to the sound of gunfire and rockets exploding less than a block away.

There we began our wait for word from Chairman Arafat's offices.

And we waited, hearing gunfire nearby.

159

And we waited...

And we waited some more...

Nothing was certain. I'm sure Joe, Sheryl and I silently grew more anxious as the minutes and hours ticked away. I didn't think Hisham shared our angst.

* * * * *

We waited anxiously nearly several hours for a message from Chairman Arafat's Beirut offices to find out if and when we could meet with him. Every hour increased our stress and anxiety.

"This has been a long day," Sheryl whispered, "It's hard to believe we met with President Assad in Damascus earlier today, isn't it?"

Adrenalin was racing through our veins. Nervous? Yes, of course, especially with the double issues surrounding us: the fighting in the streets nearby and the impending meeting with the man so hated by Israel.

When we asked Hisham when we would hear from the PLO, he replied tersely, "When they are certain he will meet with us," he smiled, knowingly.

Beirut: Chairman Yassir Arafat emphasizing a point to
Sandy Simon

* * * * *

After dark, at eight o'clock that same evening, I went to the
dining room table where there were many telephones. I wanted to call
my Uncle Milhelm, my father's brother, in Douma, my father's village in
the north area of Mount Lebanon, and my elderly cousin Julié Azar who
lived in Beirut.

"Which phone should I use? There are six of them." I smiled,

161

"Why six?"

Hisham shrugged, "There is so much damage to the system here in Beirut, so try them all until one catches a circuit that works. We are in the middle of a civil war."

"What is so civil about a war?" Sheryl responded in a whisper.

Now having six telephones made sense, especially for someone like me who loved to talk on the phone! I laughed at the thought, and started dialing on the nearest phone.

I wanted to speak with my father's brother Milhelm whom my father had not seen since he left Lebanon in 1920. Or, maybe Milhelm's sons Hanna and Nicola. No one in the two families had seen each other all those years except when my parents visited in 1955 to celebrate the one hundredth anniversary of the first Lebanese to emigrate to the United States. Cousin Julié had come to visit my family in Florida in 1946 and visited my third grade class in school to tell us about Lebanon. So, I was anxious to speak with her, an important link with my family and the past. On the fifth try, I was able to reach Julié. She was so excited she said she would come to our condominium apartment right away.

"No, Julié," I urged, "it's too dangerous for a woman to be walking alone in Beirut after dark."

"It's dangerous for a lady to walk alone after dark in New York City, Sandy," she laughed, expressing the eternal optimism and pride of the Lebanese. "I'll be fine. I'm close to where you are. I'll be over very soon."

I couldn't believe it when in less than twenty minutes there was a knock at the door. We jumped again.

"Who could that be?" Sheryl asked, wondering if the PLO people were back.

"Sandy!" Julié yelled to me with her slight Arabic accent from the corridor as she knocked again. I opened the door in a rush, and Cousin Julié walked in confidently carrying two large bags. She was probably sixty-five years old, maybe five feet, two inches tall.

"You've shrunk cousin," I joked. "Did the war make you shorter? What did you bring, Julié?" I was so happy to see my cousin after so many years.

"You have to have something to eat," she laughed, "so I brought you cheese, rolled grape leaves, hummus, zeytoon, olives, khubbus, bread, and even some kibbee!"

"Kibbee too? You are incredible, cousin! How did you get here so fast?"

"Well, I live just around the corner. It was easy for me."

"You live in West Beirut where all the fighting is! Are you crazy?"

"Yes, of course, but I love West Beirut. I've lived here for thirty years. And with the PLO here, West Beirut is the safest, best protected area of Beirut, Sandy. For many years it has been known as a place for poets, intellectuals, and Bohemians. Like The Village in New York. But now it's difficult because West Beirut is being destroyed by this war. Because of the Israelis, the poor Palestinians have no place else to go. But now, we have Maronite Christian militias, mostly led by the

163

powerful Chamoun and Gemayel families fighting the Palestinians, mostly Muslims in an effort to drive all Palestinians out of Lebanon. The Gemayel family militia has aligned with the Israelis. Bashir Gemayel wants to become President. Many fear if he wins, he will align Lebanon with Israel and Lebanon will remain the battleground of the Middle East for years to come."

"But Beirut thrives only under peace!" Sheryl commented, sad as I was to hear these details. "Julié, you must be very sad, cousin."

"Sandy, I am very sad and I am very angry at Gemayel, Chamoun, the Israelis and the Palestinians. They are destroying our beautiful city ... our country, wonderful Lebanon! They don't want the PLO here in Beirut because Israel will do all it can to destroy the PLO no matter where they locate. We don't want all these Palestinians in Lebanon and they don't want to be here. They want to go home to their own state. Why can't the U.S. make that happen?"

We hugged again, sat down and, for about an hour, happily talked about life in Beirut during the war, and about our family in in Douma, safely in the northern mountains.

"The family is safe in the mountains, Sandy. There has been no fighting near Douma."

"Thank God. I wish I was able to get there or at least speak with Uncle Milhelm."

"I'm sorry. You can't go there. Normally, it's only an hour drive, but now it's not possible. Too many people with guns. But," she hastened to add, "they called me and told me they saw you all on the TV when you met with President Sarkis. You have made the family very proud, very happy. Uncle Milhelm was so proud to see you. He cried and told me you look just like your father."

Around ten o'clock, Julié reluctantly left, although she passionately asked if she could go with us to meet and thank Chairman Arafat. She felt that way because the PLO had established safety in her neighborhood and West Beirut. And she hated that Israel had invaded Lebanon and still occupied much of South Lebanon. There were so many militias fighting each other, and each had their own safe zones.

Julié's visit brought us all to the reality of the war and our visit helped us understand it better during such a bad time.

"You must come back when we are not at war. You will love Beirut. It's such an exciting city."

After she left us, we returned to waiting, excited with anticipation, yet, for some reason, maybe because Julié put the situation in a better perspective, We seemed less afraid, even while listening to the street fighting going on outside only a short distance from our "safe house." We heard a constant barrage of automatic machine guns firing, and the occasional rocket blasts against buildings in the city, mostly near the green line. It was unnerving to all of us who certainly were not accustomed to being in a veritable war zone, and in a city always known for its *joie de vivre* and freedom of movement.

"How do you feel about this meeting tonight?" I asked Sheryl as she sat looking at our notes from our previous meetings throughout the Arab world.

"I'm surprised, Sandy, that I'm not at all afraid. I somehow feel very good about our mission, and tonight we visit with Chairman

Arafat! It's all very exciting. I actually feel very safe, but I must admit I'm also terrified," she laughed. "Go figure!" and she laughed again. "We sure enjoyed your cousin's visit. I just love her and her *tabouli* and hummus."

"I feel the same way. I mean I'm amazed with this entire trip. There are so many contrasts, so many contradictions of what our media and politicians feed us. Being warmly welcomed by King Hussein in his home! And King Khalid in Riyadh! I can hardly believe all the heads of state spent so much time with us."

"And always serving us tea and orange juice before discussing the terrible political situation all over the Middle East," Sheryl added.

"How do you explain that the United States has had absolutely no dialogue with those countries in weeks? None whatever! And here we have been all these leaders for at least three hours each, and received with open arms and extraordinary friendliness. They love Americans, but totally reject our government's policies, another contrast or dichotomy."

Joe Baroody joined in the conversation, saying, "Even President Assad of Syria spent many hours with us explaining in great detail the Arab perspectives. Most notably, Syria's. It was clear from all the heads of state who have had no official communication with the U.S. government that they were very angry at our government and upset about those unilateral negotiations between Israel and Egypt."

He thought a moment then continued, "They would greatly prefer full, unequivocal U.S. support for a regional peace treaty, and adamantly felt the U.S. was ignoring the plight of the Palestinian people who deserve human rights and their own state. They believe the U.S.

government is hypocritical when they state they stand for human rights, yet ignore the plight of the Palestinians."

"Yet," Hisham reiterated, "I agree they all love and respect Americans and America. They just don't like our government's actions in the Middle East. And don't forget, Egypt by far is the most populated and most powerful Arab country. If they sign this treaty with Israel, while there may be no regional war in the Middle East, I can definitely assure you that without a provision for a Palestine state, there will be no peace for Israel or anyone else."

"And," Sheryl added, "to achieve peace and allow a Palestinian state would be in Israel's best interests. That's what puzzles me about the rigid stance of the Likud Party. Think of the incredible opportunities of tourism, jobs, high tech research, and an enormous amount of wealth aside from oil. Everybody wins in my view!"

"You are right, Sheryl," I replied. "When someone has no hope and believes neither they nor their children have a future, they will become desperate. And desperate people do desperate things."

"I thought it interesting," Joe reminded us, "at least President Assad, during our meetings, told us, 'We Arabs did not belong in Spain, (recalling the Moorish invasion and occupation of Spain for 500 hundred years). Eventually, Europe kicked the Muslims out. I believe he told us that, while it may take 100 or 500 years, the Zionist's state will become a secular state, not a Jewish state, and the Zionist entity (his term) will disappear. We will out populate them, build more schools, more hospitals, and educate more Arabs. It's just a matter of time, and it will not require another war.'"

We had a good and enlightening two way conversation going

167

and I added, "I thought it significant too that President Assad said the Arabs don't hate Jews. He did say many times the Arabs completely oppose the goals, policies and actions of the Zionists. As a matter of fact, it seems to us that the Muslim world clearly differentiates Zionism from Judaism. And that they empathize with the Jews."

"Jewish people were treated so badly over the centuries in Christian Europe.

"Those inquisitions and the Holocaust weren't Christian beliefs. The faith was abandoned and replaced by hate and discrimination, totally opposite of true Christian beliefs."

Joe interceded, "That is what the Arabs believe Zionism has done to Judaism, which they and we believe is the root of Christianity and Islam faiths. After all, Jesus was a Jew."

"And," Hisham added, "the Koran clearly states Muslims believe Abraham is their ancestor too. It also clearly considers Moses, Elijah and Jesus to be prophets."

"So what is the problem?"

Hisham quickly responded, "The problem is Zionism, not the Jewish faith or Jews per se."

"But what is the difference between Judaism and Zionism?"

"Judaism is the belief, as I understand it, the following of the laws of Moses, The Torah, and by doing that, a Jew becomes one with God.

"And, Zionism is a movement begun in the nineteenth century to establish a Jewish homeland in Palestine, which they consider their ancient homeland of Israel as formed by King David when he united the twelve tribes of Israel. There was a great deal of opposition to creating a Jewish state by displacing a people, but in the end, most Jews now support the policies of taking all lands they believe God gave to Abraham thousands of years ago."

"But Abraham is the ancestor of all people the world over, Christians and Muslims believe."

"So, what is the best means of bringing these two belligerents together?"

"Perhaps if they both actually follow the tenets of their respective religions, they would find peace. They both need to reject violence for the other side to soften their position."

"But the Zionist goal is predicated on Palestine for Jews only, no other people need apply," Hisham declared emphatically, with a bit of anger.

Shifting our discussion, we agreed that was a profound statement from President Assad who firmly believes Syria should remain a secular state, providing protection, security and freedom for minorities. Much like Ataturk established in Turkey earlier in the 1920s.

"I was very impressed with President Assad," commented Hisham. "I felt he was very fair in his, his comments and his vision, especially for the self-determination of the Palestinian people and for a regional peace agreement."

We agreed in our conversations that we were quite impressed with our career ambassadors, especially in Jordan, Qatar and Syria on our fact-finding mission. U.S. ambassadors were not available in

Bahrain, Qatar, Iraq, Lebanon or Saudi Arabia. Ambassador Veliotes, Andrew Killgore in Doha, Qatar, and Talcott Seeley in Damascus, spoke fluent Arabic, which enabled them to bridge cultural differences with those government leaders, which facilitated an ease of accomplishing their difficult missions. All three were most capable, hospitable, and keenly interested in our mission and what we learned during our interviews. They lived with the stressful situation existing between the Arab countries and Israel, and America's position as interpreted by the Arab governments.1967.

"Remember," Sheryl said, "how gracious King Hussein was when he led us into his beautiful, spacious living room, served us tea, and apologized that Queen Noor could not join us because she was preparing for their trip to the United States?"

He invited us to join him at the window and said, "You see there, looking through the large windows," the King gestured, "that we can see Jerusalem from this hilltop. It is just twenty miles to the west. It is agonizing for our people to be so close, yet prohibited by the Israelis."

* * * * *

As we anxiously awaited the message that we were to see Chairman Arafat, we looked at each other often. Sheryl and I exchanged thoughts: *Would he be alone when we met? Who else would we meet with? Where?*

We were imbedded in West Beirut in the neighborhoods

controlled by the PLO, but did not know if the fighting we heard outside would impact our ability to meet with him or if getting to his offices was safe.

And, we wondered a bit anxiously, what would he say about the Egypt-Israel peace agreement and how it affects the PLO, the Palestinian people, the possibilities of a Palestinian state or, we wondered, would Israel and the PLO continue their war? Would there be a call for another intifada? Street riots? Bombings?

All these thoughts were going through our minds and in our conversations as we continued our vigil, awaiting word.

* * * * *

At precisely 11 p.m., we heard a sharp rap at the door.

"Who is it?" quickly asked Hisham, also a member of the PLO Congress, who had met with PLO representatives earlier that day to arrange our meeting.

What seemed a very long minute later, a man outside the door responded and stated loudly in a deep masculine voice, "We are from the PLO."

"Please come in," replied Hisham, as he opened the door.

Two men in dark suits, unarmed, wearing the black and white checkered kiffeyehs, entered our apartment.

"*Shou?*" (What?) Hisham asked.

171

"We have come to tell you that Chairman Arafat will be pleased to meet with you tonight. You will be picked up in one hour. He is flying into Beirut from Tunis and should be landing as we speak."

We were relieved, excited, and anxious to meet with Arafat, a key person in the Middle East equation.

* * * * *

At twelve midnight, after one hour exactly, we jumped in our chairs as we heard a strong double knock at the door.

Hisham quickly went to the door, opened it and welcomed two dark-haired, mustached, unarmed men in suits. Immediately, after seeing Hisham whom they had met earlier in the day, they stepped in and announced, "The Chairman will see you now. Please come with us."

Sheryl and I looked at each other, both thinking, "Well, for better or worse, we are about to meet with the man much of the U.S. and its government opposed, labeling him a leader of a terrorist organization who, at the time, was not even permitted in the U.S.

As Lebanese-Americans, we did not agree with our nation's stance because of our empathy for the injustices borne by the Palestinian and Lebanese people for more than thirty years. But we also opposed the continuing bombings and cruelty from both sides.

"An eye for an eye, a tooth for a tooth ... if it never stops," Sheryl whispered to me. "They'll all be blind and toothless! That's insane!"

172

We quickly followed our escorts to the elevator, then down to the small lobby where we came face to face with two bearded men wearing black and white checkered kiffeyehs, a la Arafat, holding automatic assault weapons. The four men led us to two small, black, four-door Toyota sedans. One armed guard got into the front passenger seat as Hisham and Joe sat in the back seat of the first car. Sheryl and I were led to the second black Toyota, also four-door. Our armed guard also sat in the front passenger seat next to our driver.

"Scared?" I asked Sheryl as she sat close to me.

"A little I guess, but I feel well-protected although we're going into the unknown."

Then, after we passed the first sandbagged checkpoint with a group of heavily armed guards, Sheryl whispered to me, "Are we out of our minds?"

I laughed and replied, "I guess we are, but we didn't know we'd be here, did we? We'll just have to trust in the Lord, Sheryl. We are going where few, if any Americans, have gone before. But I think it's very exciting!"

We were surprised that the two cars left the apartment building in opposite directions, thinking we would have been safer trailing Hisham's car.

"Where are we going?"

Silence from the front seat as we wove through the labyrinth of narrow, almost ancient streets of old West Beirut, winding, turning, it seemed at every possible intersection. A few times, we made quick U-turns. At each turn or U-turn, we saw on both sides of the street paramilitary personnel standing with their automatic assault rifles at the ready, protected by stacks of sandbags. As we approached each checkpoint, our guard in the front seat would speak orders to the driver who responded with a turn, or he slowed down, receiving a "clear passage" from the armed sentinels. We must have come to at least a dozen dark checkpoints during our thirty minute drive. It was in total midnight darkness that we drove, no lights in the car, no street lights, no flashlights, just armed checkpoints reinforcing the sense of war, of impending danger at any second. We felt like we were in a Hollywood movie. But this, we remembered, was real, and the danger was real.

We passed what appeared to be threatening, dangerous, armed men wearing black and white checkered kiffeyehs, covering their entire heads except for their eyes.

At first sight of each sandbagged checkpoint, neither of us knew if they were "on our side," whatever side we were on, we did not know.

Neither of us had experienced such drama, such possible impending danger. After all, there had been reported multiple kidnappings as revenge or for a ransom.

"We're here on a mission, Sandy, for the President of the United States! Surely no one would want to kidnap us!" She paused, then looked at me and continued softly, "Or would they?"

I could see her eyes filling with tears as the reality of our situation and its potential for us to be taken, shot, killed or kidnapped finally struck us.

"Well, Sheryl," I replied nervously as I tried to stay calm and confident, "if they want us for any reason, this is their best opportunity!"

"Is that supposed to make me laugh?" Sheryl anxiously replied.

"We're okay, Sheryl. It's been thirty minutes since we left the apartment," I commented as I checked my watch.

"Thirty minutes? That's all? It seems like we've been driving for hours!"

"It sure does, Sheryl. I mean, we must have made at least four U-turns and a dozen other turns. It's so eerily completely dark!"

"We've passed nine armed checkpoints!"

"Arafat sure is protected, isn't he?"

* * * * *

Finally, at 1 a.m., our car pulled up in front of a condominium much like ours. There was space in front for four small cars, then a lobby/passageway into the building leading straight to the single elevator.

As we stepped out of the car, we were kindly assisted by the guards,(*another sharp contrast*, I thought, *so gracious and respectful*), we were escorted into the building surrounded by four men wearing their kiffeyehs covering all but their eyes, sinister looking to be sure, but gracious, yet always looking around for danger.

When we reached the elevator, one pressed the "up" button.

175

We stood at the elevator when the door opened. Inside were two guards armed with automatic assault rifles aimed directly at Sheryl and me. I thought to myself, *if anyone makes a wrong move, we will surely be victims of a deadly blood bath, shot each at least twenty times.*

This moment is one I will never forget. It was, of course, a first in both our lives to be that close to certain death.

To read about people being shot, maimed, or killed is one thing, but to be personally confronted with that possibility only inches from the end of two assault machine guns is quite startling and frightening.

The guards stepped aside, inviting us into the elevator. Two armed guards stood on either side of Sheryl and me as we rode up, their guns aimed at the elevator door. At the fifth floor, the door automatically opened. Instantly, we faced two more armed guards holding their assault weapon at the ready, aimed directly at us. Another potential assassination? Another possible blood bath? Yes. We faced those possibilities as we began to understand the lives these Palestinian resistance forces and, especially Yassir Arafat, faced every single day, driven from their homes with no place to go. We had been told that Chairman Arafat never slept in the same place twice in a row. *What a way to live,* I thought. Why? *Because he led the fight for his people to return to their homes.*

It seemed another major contrast as we were politely escorted down the lighted hallway into a small waiting room with a table and four chairs where Hisham and Joe sat, awaiting our arrival.

In perhaps two minutes, a staff member in guerrilla clothes approached, entered the room carrying a silver service tray on which there were small glasses of orange juice, water, and cups of hot tea, lemon wedges, spoons, and a sugar cup.

What irony! Every moment seemed filled with dichotomy all the time.

We had just experienced what could easily have been our last ride in a car, passed armed guards behind stacked sandbags, heard gunfire in the near distance, faced assault machinegun guards at every juncture of our journey to PLO headquarters deeply imbedded in the West Beirut war zone, and now we are presented a tray of orange juice, water and tea! (Scotch would have calmed our nerves!)

How could this be? I asked myself. An oxymoron, a metaphor, a contradiction of all we ever learned from the U.S. media.

* * * * *

"The Chairman will see you now," announced the second staff member as he entered our waiting room. We all smiled, excitedly looking forward to sitting face to face with this bearded "terrorist" that the U.S. and Israeli governments hated so much, the individual who the U.S. media castigated daily, convincing most Americans that Israelis were righteous, while Palestinians were stereotyped as terrorists, roaches, and any other pejorative term available. As we entered Chairman Arafat's modest office, he stepped from behind his modest, wooden desk, spread his arms and, with his characteristic broad smile, welcomed us individually with an embrace, and gestured to the four chairs opposite him across his simple wood desk.

My God, I thought, *will the contradictions of what we are fed in America by our politicians and media ever end? We are barraged daily! There has to be a better way. These are human beings driven from their farms, their homes.*

As I was the only person with a camera this time, I began taking photographs. But I remembered Hisham yelling at me in the drive from the airport: "Put down that camera! They will stop us and arrest us as spies and confiscate your camera!"

As I began putting away my camera, Arafat gestured and spoke to me, "No, please, take all the photographs you wish. You are our brothers. Please sit there." He pointed to the chair directly opposite him. In the end, I took an entire roll of thirty-six photographs of Chairman Arafat while he was speaking, sometimes gesturing with his index finger pointing to the ceiling to make a point. I also took photographs of the four middle-aged advisers sitting to our left.

For the next two hours ... two hours! ... we listened to Yassir Arafat describe the historical journey of the Palestinian people from when the early Philistines lived in Gaza and Canaan, then in greater detail beginning in the late nineteenth century when the Zionist movement began sending European immigrants to Palestine. He described how at first there were not so many Jews coming and how they were accepted throughout the 1920s and 1930s.

"And then, the Germans attacked the Jews! Our brothers in Abraham! How could Hitler do such a terrible thing? How could the world, especially the powerful United States, do nothing?

"All went fairly well until the British abandoned Palestine, and they, with England's acquiescence and President Truman, decided to secure the Jewish vote in the 1947 election by strongly encouraging England to permit not 15,000 Jewish immigrants each year, but increase the number to 100,000 each year, while the United States would not permit European Jews to enter the United States. Unbelievable! Unbelievable!" he reiterated. "Palestine is a very small country. To receive hundreds of thousands of people who are different, with different cultures into a land of peaceful farmers, olive and citrus growers, is insanity! A script for resentment! Invented and imposed on us by the U.S. and England.

"Once we were a people with a country, human rights, and hopes for a good future for our children. Now we find ourselves rooted out of our homes, farms, offices, olive groves, cities, and villages. Most are now living our lives in poverty as refugees in other countries, driven out by a people without a country, who were driven out of Europe. Now we are faced with a mostly Western world uncaring and completely supportive of the aggressors and their cruel policies!

"Today, the Palestinian people are exempted from all the Western discourse urging human rights across the globe, especially by the politicians in Washington.

"We are a people whose land has been taken arbitrarily by a harsh, extremist Zionist government enforcing apartheid in the West Bank.

"We have no tanks, no jet fighters, no armored vehicles, no guns to match Israel's Western supplied arms, who for several early years were armed by Czechoslovakia and other Soviet bloc nations.

"We have only one determination, with the power of faith in God, Allah, and the blood of our sons. It is a horrible thing to seek a return to our homes, our orchards, our farms with nothing but stones and sticks. And, even though the Zionists terrorize our people daily, we are forced to live under Israel's military occupation of the last twenty percent of Palestine. Even though Israel breaks every agreement, and denies U.N. resolutions, we are the people who are cursed and labeled 'terrorists.'

"It is much like when the Spanish colonized the Western hemisphere. They demeaned them, identified them as a lesser people and as a result, invited the Europeans to turn them into slaves, to slaughter them and take their homeland. Colonialism there is the same as Zionist Israel's colonialism of Palestine. It is wrong, inhuman, and we will fight for our rights as human beings and a Palestinian homeland for our people until we are all dead. We will never, ever, ever give up, as Winston Churchill urged his people during World War II. We will fight with stones, with sticks, and face their beatings and their U.S. tanks until we have our homeland, our state, our honor and self-esteem for us and our children.

"This," he said, pointing his index finger upward for emphasis, "is what we must do. And with the help of God Almighty, we will succeed if it takes one hundred years. Israel cannot continue on its inhumane path!"

"How do you feel about the Camp David Accords between Egypt and Israel?" Joe asked.

Arafat's demeanor changed to anger from determination. "Sadat is a stupid, stupid man, and a traitor to the Arab world. He became convinced by the Western media that he was a hero, and hoped the Egyptian people would change their opinion of him, an appointed, not elected leader, from a cruel despot to a world leader. It will not happen.

"Sadat allowed the Israelis to remove the most populated, the most heavily armed Arab country, Egypt, to surrender, removing even a semblance of balance of power with Israel. And for what? All he received was the Sinai Peninsula, a barren desert. He did not include the other lands taken illegally by the Israelis in 1967! I speak about the West Bank, the Syrian Golan, the Syrians who lived there, and East Jerusalem, holy to all Muslims.

"He got a hell hole of a desert, promises of billions of dollars, although only a tiny portion of what Israel will receive from the U.S. He has turned his back on his brothers and sisters. He has no honor, no allies. He is a pariah. And no other Arab country will participate in such an agreement."

Pointing his finger again, he added, "We all wish for peace in our lifetime— but with honor. We wish for a Palestinian state in the West Bank, our capital in East Jerusalem, the Golan returned to Syria and the evacuation of the Israelis from our lands. Then, and only then, will the Arab world come to a peace agreement with Israel. But Israel refuses to agree with those terms."

"But how can you defeat the Israelis with all their Western aid and their unwillingness to seek peace?" Sheryl asked.

"We will seek peace at any time. We will do it with honor and keep our word. It is our culture. But as long as we are oppressed and suffer at the points of their bayonets, we will fight back. We do not hate Jews. We want equality, human rights. We and the Jewish people are both from the seed of Abraham. Ishmael and Isaac were brothers. We too are brothers, but we cannot live like this without a homeland. Only the U.S. can make Israel accept peace and Palestinian human rights. But they are servants of the Israeli political lobbyists, so America's voice is hollow when they speak about global human rights."

Hanging on the wall behind the Chairman was a framed copper map of Palestine. When I first saw it as we entered, I wondered why he had a picture of Israel on his wall. It looked like a map of Israel as we see in our media. The two are precisely the same. Two peoples fighting, killing over the same exact lands.

* * * * *

From impressions given us daily on television and from our politicians in Washington, by 1978, most Americans and Israelis had become convinced that Chairman Yassir Arafat was an evil man, a terrorist, a person, along with those he represented, to be hated and scorned.

Indeed, he looked like the images we'd been shown time and again, with his seemingly unshaven face covered with what appeared to be a three-day-old beard, and his head covered in the Arab styled checkered kiffeyeh. But to our surprise, we found him to be a warm, caring, cordial, charming man.

As he began speaking to us, it was clear he was intelligent, articulate, and dedicated to the welfare of his people, the Palestinians. He was also quite knowledgeable about U.S. politics, Europe's positions and the struggle he and his people faced. He believed passionately in his cause to seek the return of lands indigenous people owned and occupied for many, many centuries, even before Moses and Joshua's arrival, lands occupied and farmed by the same families, generation after generation for hundreds of years.

"Now," he continued, "the Zionists occupy all of Palestine, since in 1967 they invaded the West Bank, Gaza, the Syrian Golan, and East Jerusalem. As a result, nearly all Palestinians are refugees! Why? Why does the world allow such a thing? The world is supposed to be more civilized, with international laws to prevent colonialism, the illegal taking of other people's lands, homes, olive groves, and fruit orchards. "And now, the Zionists from all over Europe come here, take our lands, kill and beat our people, and crush our homes with bulldozers, tanks and aerial rockets sent to them by the United States and France. Why are they allowed to do such things?

"When the Native Americans fought back, the Spanish, English, and other European invaders crushed them and justified their actions by demeaning them as savages, a label is still used five hundred years later. That is the same treatment of the Palestinians whose sin was only that of living and working where the European Zionist colonialists came to occupy these lands.

"The Palestinian people played no part in the dreadful Russian progroms or the disgusting Holocaust in Europe. Germany and France carried out that tragedy. Arabs had no role in that. But the Arabs, mostly from Saudi Arabia, did provide vital oil to the Americans, all they needed, to win the war. And for that we Arabs must suffer? Why?"

He was speaking of all the injustices, including all Arabs of extended families and loyalties and wanted us to hear his message.

As we sat almost spellbound by what he was saying, none of

which could be denied, we felt as guilty as if Germans were forced to listen to the Jewish people in 1944, pleading their own case.

I looked to my left into the eyes of the six middle-aged advisors of Arafat as they sat quietly listening, nodding in agreement with his statements. We were never introduced to them and only assumed they were among his smallest circle of advisors.

With his right forefinger, pointing skyward for emphasis, he continued his presentation. "Please ask your President Carter, in my opinion, a very good man who speaks of human rights, why the Palestinian people are excluded from having God-given rights to live in freedom, the right to come and go in their own land. Why must we be forced to battle the Israelis with stones and sticks and, yes, small bombs by our very angry extremists in opposition to their world class air force, tanks, aerial rockets, and bulldozers? Why? Why do Americans treat us like trash?

"Because we are in the way of those occupiers?"

"There is no justice in Israel's taking all of our lands, causing millions of Palestinians to live like animals in refugee camps in foreign countries. I thank Allah for the generosity of our fellow Arab countries who have received us with open arms: Lebanon, Syria, Iraq, Kuwait, Bahrain, Qatar, Saudi Arabia, and more. But we want, we demand, freedom from our oppressors, the Israelis. And why should we not have that? We want peace with Israel, peace throughout the region so our children and grandchildren can have the rights all people should have."

"How," I asked, "Chairman Arafat, will you achieve that peace when the PLO sends young men to fight the Israelis? Is it possible to seek peace in a non-violent way like Gandhi did with the English in

India? Is there any other way?" I asked, then continued, "In the United States you and the PLO are depicted only as violent terrorists killing civilian Israelis, and so the American people who read the local media have come to believe this as truth."

He looked me straight in my eyes and replied, "Mr. Simon, we must fight these people. They break every agreement. They ignore U.N. Resolutions 338 and 242. And they do not even consider a Palestinian state on the tiny West Bank, just twenty percent of Palestine, during those Camp David negotiations. As a result, Anwar Sadat gave up everything and in return for becoming neutralized; the largest, best armed, most populated Arab nation only got the Sinai desert. What good is that toward peace in the entire Middle East? He is a fool, a traitor, and to be ignored. How would the Americans have responded if France alone signed a peace treaty with Hitler? It may have relieved France of Germany's occupation, but what about England, Belgium, the Baltics, Russia, Holland? How would they survive?

"There can only be an overall peace in the Middle East. No other Arab country will sign such an agreement. Sadat and Egypt will stand alone, and now, the Arab-Israeli balance of power is badly skewed even more to the Israelis.

"They have many atomic bombs, the third largest military in the world, and they use Western arms to kill and injure civilian men, women and children in Palestine, Lebanon, and Syria every day!"

Then, as though to summarize his position, he declared, "If we can obtain even just the West Bank to call our own country, our own nation, with our own passports, our honor, our flag, Israel would achieve the security they claim they want. Security cannot be obtained for Israel without an overall peace agreement!

"My life is dedicated to that accomplishment. We do not want to harm or kill anyone. Fatah, our organization, understands we are in an armed conflict, that we are far from equal in arms, but we are passionate in seeking peace and our own homeland!"

We found ourselves listening intently across his desk as the Chairman pleaded his case, unable to disagree with his goals.

I did ask him again if he could obtain a truce with Israel so to end the armed conflict to allow other forces to bring Israel to the negotiating table.

He replied, "We all were engaged for months in Geneva, negotiating a comprehensive peace treaty with all the nations in the Middle East, but, as you know, Israel and Egypt abandoned those negotiations and secretly negotiated their own unilateral agreement, something Sadat wanted for his own political standing in Egypt because he was not that popular at the time. Now, he has become hated by many in Egypt. Israel abandoned the talks because they knew they would have to return to the pre-1967 borders, to return the Golan to Syria, de-annex East Jerusalem, and stop the settlements in the West Bank, Gaza, and the Golan. They simply wanted to remove Egypt from the equation. And with U.S. support, they achieved that at no cost.

"Do you know Menachem Begin, who signed the Accords as Prime Minister of Israel, was the worst terrorist in the Middle East? As a leader of the horrible Irgun Gang, he slaughtered thousands of helpless Palestinian women and children in Deir Yassin. Even Albert Einstein and many other prominent American Jews rejected Begin. Now, in America, along with Sadat, he is a hero!

"Have you read the so-called Camp David Accords? Have you

seen that the Camp David Accords became a financial bonanza for Israel? Israel is to receive at least three billion dollars each year for arms! Three billion! Egypt's military is to receive $1.5 billion each year. Who is Israel going to use those arms against? The Palestinians? The Syrians?

"And the Egyptians. Who are they going to use their $1.5 billion in arms against? The Egyptian people to keep Sadat in power? Certainly neither will use those arms against each other now."

He continued, now, focusing on the Camp David Accords, "Are your Senators and Congressmen aware the U.S. has agreed to replace Israel's new air fields and oil drilling sites in the Sinai and rebuild them all in the Negev at U.S. taxpayers' expense in southern Israel? How many years will the U.S. pay tribute to Israel's armed forces, to Egypt's army? Thirty years? Forty years? The U.S. even guarantees Israel all the oil it needs if there is ever a shortage.

"Our people tell me only one U.S. Senator even obtained a copy of the signed Accords. Only one! They don't appear to us to represent the American people. They really vote to protect the interests of the Israelis and their own political power. Tell your President for us this simple thing: Arafat and the Palestinians will make peace with Israel tomorrow if we are allowed our own state on the West Bank, free of Israeli occupation, taking of our lands and East Jerusalem. I am convinced all Arab nations will agree to a peace treaty with Israel for the return to the 1967 borders so we can live in peace with honor, without the control of Israel over our people. It's as simple as that."

We were overwhelmed by the statements we were hearing, and we came to the conclusion that Chairman Arafat was passionate about peace, and sincere in his message we were to carry back to

Washington.

"Is there a better path to peace and establishing a Palestinian state in the West Bank and Gaza?" I asked the Chairman. "I mean, sir, can both sides stop the violence? In America, the media declare the Israeli view that their attacks are retaliatory and that the violence of bombings and the like are the cause for Israelis not trusting the Arab world. What do you think would happen if the Arab side called a truce to stop the violence? In the end, given a Palestinian state, both Palestine and Israel would be required to reject violence against one another."

"You make a valid point, Mr. Simon. Of course should the Israelis accept a Palestinian state as a reality as I described, we would so greatly appreciate that blessing we would have no need whatever to attack Israel. We would hope the two states would have full commercial, diplomatic and personal relations. We are all sons and daughters of Abraham. We are cousins! But Israel never stops bombarding our people, taking our private lands and ruling our lives that we can only stop our efforts to get back to our homes when Israel stops its violence. And as you know, even as we sit here together, Israel occupies south Lebanon and provides weapons to militias right here in Beirut."

After three hours, our very candid, informative meeting from the man himself was concluded. We felt we had nearly completed our mission, short of preparing our report to Secretary Vance.

We were filled with a sense of accomplishment, excitement, still wary for our safety until we landed in America and a feeling of privilege to represent our country at all these meetings with heads of states at a time when U.S. interests in the Middle East, aside from

188

Israel, hit a new low, creating much ill will, especially among those who already felt enmity toward the U.S. government and Israel for robbing the human rights of the Palestinian people. Many in the Muslim and Arab worlds also opposed U.S. military presence in certain Arab countries. This anger at the United States because of its financing of the Israel military might, taking of Arab lands on the West Bank, Gaza, Jerusalem, and Syria, as well as interfering in the politics of Lebanon, occupying the south 20% of Lebanon, it seemed to us, surely would generate anti-U.S. activity that would lead to U.S. interests throughout the world being threatened by those Arabs frustrated with the injustices placed on them mostly by America's client state, Israel.

* * * * *

As we left our meeting with Chairman Arafat, we conveyed our deep appreciation for his candid, personal respect, and his passionate desires for a Palestinian state, and human rights for the Palestinian people, especially the children. We embraced individually, as was the culture, kissing cheeks and saying our goodbyes. I took photos of each embrace.

We returned to the well-guarded elevator, rode down to the lobby accompanied by two heavily armed guards, and, again, as the doors opened, two guards armed with automatic assault rifles faced us. Once again, we felt one small move could cause a literal bloodbath. But we were led to our two cars, got in, and experienced another drive of at least thirty minutes, winding through the narrow streets of West Beirut, passing, and acknowledging with waves by our guard, numerous checkpoints of stacked sandbags, heavily armed guards, snipers on rooftops at many intersections, until we were safely returned to our condo apartment from whence we began. The stark contrasts of gunfire, political polemics, juxtaposed with the kindness, gentleness and friendship struck us all.

But it was late now, and with the city totally, here was little gunfire, much quieter in the city.

* * * * *

We knew our message to Secretary Cyrus Vance and President Jimmy Carter would not be what they wanted to hear. But we knew we had to carry to them the candid messages we received.

Through the U.S. State Department and Hisham's contacts, all our hosts were informed prior to our arrival of the purpose of our mission and, as Arab Americans, they felt we were representing all Americans of Arabic heritage to learn the views and position of the Arab countries following the Egypt-Israeli accord As top officials of the National Association of Arab Americans, we were trusted not only by all the government leaders we visited, but also by Secretary Vance and the Carter Administration. And we knew our report to Secretary Vance had to be concise, true and comprehensive, to be used in future decision making by the United States.

Chapter 13
Returning Home

It was about 4:30 a.m. when we arrived back at our safe house, excited, adrenalin surging through our veins, but, to be sure, getting tired after a very long day.

We discussed and re-examined our fourteen-day fact-finding mission, writing notes to assure we had everyone's perspective and agreement of our ultimate message to Secretary Vance upon our return to America. We marveled at our extraordinary meetings with so many heads of state. We could hardly believe, as Americans, most of whom, like us, knew the Middle East issues and leaders solely through the media, Hollywood, politicians, and television, especially. Clearly, the U.S. media and Hollywood were not accurate at all.

Also, we wondered, as we went to meet with President Assad and Chairman Arafat: *Were we out of our minds?*

"Joe," I asked, "you and your family are very involved in Washington politics and more aware than I and maybe Sheryl who seems to know every Lebanese family in Washington. What do you think the United States should do?"

Joe chuckled softly and replied, "You know how Washington works. And I'm not revealing any secret when I say that the most important objective of every politician, Senator or House member, is to get re-elected. And siding with the Palestinians against Israel is all it would take to get defeated at their next election. So, it remains with the White House to lead the way. But that likely would not happen until the President's second and final term."

"You are so right," we all agreed, "but what can be done to break this impasse?"

"Oh," he replied knowingly, there will be another conference somewhere, someday, maybe by the next president led under the auspices of the United States, and maybe with a more moderate, liberal Labor party in Israel much can be achieved."

"You are NAAA's next president. Shouldn't we accept President Assad's invitation and those of the other leaders we met with and continue to send delegations to meet with them, perhaps including students, reporters, even Jewish leaders?"

"Good idea, Sandy. Let's pursue that approach. Maybe it could help."

Joe, a Melkite Christian, was a pretty easy going guy from a prominent Lebanese family who were active Republicans, well respected, and maybe silently hoped a Republican president could seek a Middle East peace. The Melkite Church is ancient and Eastern in its ritual, yet is part of the Roman Catholic Church universe, so he was able to see many sides of Lebanese politics.

We spent the next two hours together, forming our written report to be presented to Mr. Vance upon our return. By the time we completed our impressions, studied our verbatim notes, and discussed our amazing trip, it was after 6 a.m. in the morning.

Hisham decided to remain in Beirut. The rest of us were ready to return to our families. Joe, Sheryl, and I were driven to the Beirut airport for our last flight on the Alia Airlines' Lear jet to Amman to catch our flight to Washington via Paris.

Unfortunately, we arrived too late to catch our flight to Paris. So we had to wait for a later flight. This one took us to Frankfurt, Germany, then Paris.

We each called our families to let them know we were safe and en route home. That's how Sheryl learned her sister had given birth to a beautiful baby girl.

"My sister had a baby girl! I have a niece!" she exclaimed excitedly, then laughed, "My sister had a baby girl! I've got to get home as soon as possible!" She was so excited, so proud, and even more anxious to get back to America.

In Paris, it had been arranged, by our friend Ali Ghandour for the three of us to fly back, this time direct to Dulles Airport, outside Washington in Britain and France's pride and joy, the Concorde, an exciting supersonic jet transport, the SST that flew, we were told, at Mach 1.6,, that is 1.6 times the speed of sound, or about 1200 mph. "Look, Sandy! It's so small, but beautiful!" Sheryl exclaimed excitedly, looking out the terminal window at the parked Concorde.

"It looks kind of sexy, doesn't it?" I smiled wickedly.

As we entered the plane, we could see the aisle was much smaller than we were accustomed to in other commercial aircraft.

We settled in and while buckling our seat belts, the lovely attendants came to offer us beverages and snacks of every kind.

"This is what they call 'flying in style,' isn't it Joe?" I said to him across the aisle.

In just a few short hours we stepped on the tarmac at Dulles and Sheryl exclaimed what we all felt, "What a fantastic flight! It's good to be home!"

Our mission accomplished.

Alia Airlines Lear jet we were offered

* * * * *

Upon our return to Washington, D.C., we were honored to meet with Secretary of State Cyrus Vance for a debriefing session to report to him our findings.

During our two hour conference, we explained that *none* of the heads of state would join in the Camp David Accords without an agreement by Israel for a Palestinian state and Israel's return to the 1967 borders.

On conclusion of our report, Secretary Vance told us, "President Carter and I believe all the countries you visited truly want peace with Israel. We hope they will join in on a regional peace treaty using the

Egypt-Israel Treaty as a starting point. We expect Jordan to agree to begin negotiations with Israel, and then hopefully, the Saudis will join in, then Syria, Lebanon, and Iraq."

We replied, "There was a regional peace agreement conference in Geneva seeking that solution, they told us, but Egypt and Israel left, abandoning the negotiations."

We added, "We were told everywhere the same thing: There can be no such peace agreement until Israel agrees to a Palestinian state, self-determination, and human rights. And all Israeli settlements must be removed, restoring the 1967 borders. They were adamant."

Chapter 14
Epilogue

Throughout our mission, our discussions focused principally on the Egypt-Israel peace accord. At every meeting, we heard dire predictions that angry young Arab Muslim men would harden their anti-Israel, Anti-American rhetoric and attitudes due to the actions of the Israeli government not adhering to UN resolutions 242 and 338 and not returning lands taken during the 1967 war. As a result, we were told time and again, predictions that these young men, believing that their freedoms would never return and their lives were hopeless, would turn to the Islamist movement and vent their anger against Israel, Christians, and America. This growing animosity made them easy recruits, convincing them to join extremist organizations like Al Qaida, The Muslim Brotherhood, and the like.

Iran itself was not discussed because the Shah still governed a secular, pro-Western yet harsh regime. But the growing movement of anti-West extremism was looked on as a coming threat due to Israel's government actions.

But less than one year later, in 1979, the Shah was removed and replaced by the Islamist Revolution led by Khomeini who recanted his promises of equal freedom and removed all freedoms for women and minorities who consequently suffered greatly with rapes, killings, and imprisonment of women and Christians.

197

Some believe the Iran Islamists seek to create an Islamist Caliphate throughout the entire Middle East.

The only opposition Iran faced strong enough was the secular, U.S.-armed regime of Saddam Hussein of Iraq who favored, like Syria, Jordan, Lebanon, and other Gulf States, secular, mostly pro-Western societies.

But after September 11, 2001, the U.S., under the leadership of President Bush and Vice-President Cheney, invaded and occupied Iraq, removed the secular Ba'ath Party, and removed the only firewall opposing Iran's growing anger and terrorist actions toward Israel and the United States. Iran blamed Israel and the United States for all the abuse of fellow Muslims, especially in the West Bank, Gaza, East Jerusalem, and Syria's Golan. Iran began arming and financing Hamas in Gaza and Hezbollah in the south of Lebanon. Further, since the removal of U.S. forces in Iraq, Iran set out to expand its influence and nuclear capabilities which Israel is convinced means Iran is seeking to build an atomic bomb. Shipments of nuclear expertise and facilities from North Korea provide Iran with necessary assistance.

Christians continue to suffer throughout the Middle East. Prior to the establishment of Israel in 1948, fully twenty-eight percent (28%) of the Palestinians were Christian. Today there are only two percent (2%). Most have fled Palestine or been removed or killed.

Iran has bankrolled extremist Islamic organizations across the Middle East in Egypt and other states in Africa. To this day, Iran's policies are unpredictable and yet intent on converting all states in the Middle East to Islamic states under the rule of Sharia. Extremist Islamists believe there is to be no separation of government and the Koran.

Today, 2013, in Syria, Christians and other non-Muslims are

198

threatened with the loss of their freedoms. Women are being raped each day, threatened, and killed. Only the Bashar Al Assad government seeks to preserve Syria as a secular nation, and alone stands in the way of the "Opposition" which is comprised of extremist Islamic groups, including Al Qaida, The Muslim Brotherhood, and the Al Nousra Brigade which is from the newly named the Islamic Republic of Iraq. Most groups in the "Opposition" are external forces supported by states who do not want Syria to be a secular state. All this happening after the U.S. invasion that cost one trillion dollars, and caused death or injury to 200,000 of America's young men and women.

Yet, today, the U.S. government not only favors The Muslim Brotherhood in Egypt, resisting the moderate, Christian interim government, but supports the "Opposition" in Syria. Russia strongly supporting Assad while President Obama and supplies some groups in the Syrian "Opposition" in an effort to remove Bashar Al Assad's government.

* * * * *

After thirteen days of agonizingly frustrating intensive secret negotiations at Camp David hosted by President Jimmy Carter, President Anwar Sadat of Egypt and Prime Minister Menachem Begin of Israel signed the framework for peace between Israel and Egypt at the White House on September 17, 1978, witnessed in writing by President Carter. The signing was presented with great fanfare and viewed on television by millions worldwide. Touted as landmark peace agreement, viewers hoped these two leaders' agreement facilitated by President Carter would lead to a regional peace, finally, after three decades of wars and numerous unsuccessful U.S. efforts of shuttle diplomacy to the Middle East.

Because Sadat and Begin resented each other and would not meet in the same room or cabin, President Carter had to shuttle back and forth from Sadat's cabin to Begin's carrying counteroffers, ideas, and positions to the opposite party. How he held the negotiations together was just short of a miracle as Begin, despite President Carter's total commitment to human rights and his passionate efforts, would not, under any circumstance, recognize human rights for the Palestinian people and agree to a Palestinian state in the West Bank, taken by Israel in 1967, just eleven years earlier. In addition, Israel was taking more and more privately-owned land in the West Bank to provide ultra-right Israelis with subsidized housing in multiple settlements.

In the end, the first Accord: *A Framework for Peace in the Middle East,* went nowhere although President Carter worked feverishly to obtain both Accords, including the second Accord: *A Framework for the Conclusion of a Peace Treaty between Egypt and Israel,* believing if he succeeded, the other Arab nations would join in to bring about a regional peace. But it was not to be. Only a unilateral agreement between Israel and Egypt was completed to the chagrin of the other Arab leaders.

The second of the two agreements signed: *A Framework for the Conclusion of a Peace Treaty between Israel and Egypt* led to the 1979 Egypt-Israel Peace Treaty. As a result, President Sadat and Prime Minister Begin shared the 1978 Nobel Peace Prize.

The first agreement sought: *Camp David Accords, A Framework for Peace in the Middle East,* dealt with the Palestinian people, a possible state, and their human rights in the so-called Palestinian territories. The more important of the two, regrettably made little progress. It fell short of the hopes of President Carter, President Sadat, and the leaders of the other twenty-one Arab nations.

The Camp David Accords were the result of intensive diplomatic efforts by the U.S., Israel, and Egypt that began after President Carter took office. Several other U.S. Presidents had also sought a peace agreement between Israel and its neighbors over several decades to no avail.

President Carter felt peace in the Middle East was of critical importance to U.S. interests, and his efforts to extend human rights abroad, and placed these negotiations a high priority on this goal. His administration initially sought a comprehensive resolution between Israel and the entire Arab world. Regrettably, even during the Geneva conference on a regional peace agreement, Israel and Egypt, seeking to obtain their own singular best interests, surreptitiously began secret unilateral negotiations, abandoning the regional negotiations, which were an effort to achieve the objectives of the U.N. Security Council Resolution 242 which called for "an eventual creation of a Palestinian state in the "territories."

To his credit, President Carter made every effort to achieve a multi-national, regional peace agreement in accordance with Resolution 242. During his first year in office, he personally met with President Sadat, King Hussein of Jordan, President Assad of Syria, and Yitzak Rabin, then Prime Minister of Israel. All claimed to work toward a regional peace agreement, giving President Carter a sense of well-founded hope.

However, Begin, former member of the notorious terrorist, Zionist Irgun Gang and leader of the hardline, right wing extremist Likud Party, succeeded Rabin after Rabin was assassinated by a right wing Israeli. Begin refused to offer anything to King Hussein who initially supported Sadat's efforts. The PLO stood opposed without the possibility of a Palestinian state, which Begin and the Likud publicly rejected. President Assad told President Carter in Geneva he had no interest in negotiating with Israel as Israel actually invaded and took the Golan in 1967 *after* Syria proposed a peace treaty, and both Syria and Israel had agreed to the U.N. cease fire. Later, Israel occupied the Golan Heights and then annexed them illegally. Assad refused to come to America but agreed to meet with President Carter in Geneva. Later, he told us that he had high respect for President Carter. "He's a good man. I trust him."

President Carter's meetings convinced him to seek to reinvigorate the peace process based on the Geneva conference and U.N. Resolutions 338 and 242, and present two main objectives for an Arab-Israeli peace. First, Arab recognition of Israel's right to exist in peace, and second, Israel's withdrawal from the occupied territories taken during the June 1967 Six-Day War through negotiations to ensure Israel's security, and secure an undivided Jerusalem.

But, Begin and his hardline Likud and other extremist parties refused publicly to even discuss relinquishing control over the West Bank and East Jerusalem, holy to the Islamic world of over 12 billion people. As a result, Sadat, whose popularity in Egypt was already very low due in part to a very weak economy, high unemployment, great poverty, his control of the opposition, and lack of foreign investment, believed he could turn around his lack of popular support by making peace, albeit unilaterally, with Israel.

His judgment, as it turned out, was dramatically opposite of what actually happened. At the time of the negotiations, Egypt, like Syria, was a client state of the Soviet Union, and thus, on the opposite side from America during the waning years of the Cold War. Sadat eagerly sought to become more prominent on the global stage, more popular in Egypt, and a darling in the West, especially in the U.S. He believed that by leaving the Soviet sphere of influence and making peace with America's client Israel, America would agree to help finance an economic recovery in Egypt, securing his position as President of Egypt. But it was not to be.

* * * * *

Normalization of relations between Israel and Egypt went into effect in January, 1980. Ambassadors were exchanged in February, 1980. Boycott laws were repealed in Egypt the same month, and a degree of trade developed between the two countries, although much less than Israel hoped for. Airline flights were inaugurated in March, 1980. And for all intents and purposes, Egypt and Israel have steadfastly adhered to the unilateral agreement between the two nations.

Throughout the Middle East, the perception of Egypt, especially in the Arab world, changed dramatically. Prior to the Accords, Egypt had enormous influence as the most populated, most powerful military in the Arab world. Now withdrawn, its influence fell precipitously. Egypt was suspended from the Arab League from 1979-1989 and became irrelevant in the Arab world.

Jordan, which had exerted control over the West Bank and East Jerusalem, was left out of the negotiations, and King Hussein was highly offended. There remained "the Palestinian issues."

* * * * *

On October 6, 1981, Anwar Sadat was assassinated by Islamist fundamentalist army officers while observing a parade of the Egyptian military. But Egypt did leave the Soviet sphere and, because it made peace with Israel, America's politicians and media proclaimed Egypt a friend. And more Egyptian students were allowed, for the first time in years, to study in the United States.

Menachem Begin, Prime Minister of Israel from 1977-1983, and founder of the extreme right wing Likud Party died on March 9, 1992.

President Jimmy Carter, who served one term as President, created the Carter Center in Atlanta, Georgia, and for the past thirty years has been traveling across the globe seeking justice and preservation of human rights. Everywhere, it seems, he has been effective except in the West Bank, which is still occupied by the Israeli government.

Yitzhak Rabin, who served as Israel's Prime Minister from 1974-1977 and sought peaceful resolutions with the Palestinians during the Oslo Conference, agreed to have Israel leave the West Bank and give it back to the Palestinians. Rabin thus shared the Nobel Peace Prize with Simon Peres, Foreign Minister of Israel, and Yassir Arafat, Chairman of the PLO.

But before his re-election, he was assassinated on November 4, 1995 by a radical right wing Israeli.

* * * * *

Ariel Sharon, called "The Butcher of Lebanon and who later served as Israel's Prime Minister from 2001-2006, broke from the Likud Party and formed Kadima, a centrist political party. As Prime Minister and then a centrist, he determined it was in Israel's best interests to end its occupation of Gaza and the West Bank. Under great criticism from the right wing radicals of the Likud Party, he removed all Israeli settlers and military from Gaza and a few settler outposts from the northern West Bank. . As he was about to "clear Israel out" of the West Bank, he suffered a massive life-threatening hemorrhagic stroke on January 4, 2006. To the date of this writing, seven years later, he remains in a coma under long-term medical care at his home in the Negev desert.

* * * * *

In Israel, there remains an estimated support level of nearly 80% for the evacuation of Gaza, and the Camp David Accords. Yet, there are some who say Israel paid too high a price by giving up the oil wells Israel installed during their occupation in Sinai, its tourist-attracting geography, as well as the forced removal of extremist settlers in the Sinai. Of course, as part of the Accords, Egypt agreed to provide Israel with oil, replacing that Sinai oil production Israel returned to Egypt. Egypt continues to provide oil and gas to Israel to this day, in keeping with the Accord.

Since 1979, America has fulfilled its promise to provide to Egypt $1.3 billion annually to upgrade and sustain its military, including U.S. materiel, humanitarian grants and the like. In contrast, since the Accords, the U.S. has granted Israel $3 billion in grants and military aid packages.

And while Sadat claimed he could "deliver" Jordan to join in, the opposition in the Arab world grew so great against Sadat that Jordan could not participate without the support of its neighbors, Syria, Iraq, and Saudi Arabia, who were not interested and didn't trust Israel's Likud government to begin with. Had he joined in those circumstances, he would have become isolated and the PLO may well have caused him even more trouble.

The Accord disintegrated the united front of the Arab world and significantly tilted the balance of power to Israel, convincing their right wing extremist government to increase the taking of private lands in the West Bank, building more subsidized settlements in Syria's Golan, East Jerusalem, and the West Bank. Every expansion of settlements caused global chagrin, but not much else.

Egypt's realignment created a power vacuum that Saddam Hussein, who officially took over control of Iraq in July 1979, eight months after our meetings with Iraq's Ba'ath Party officials, believed he could fill that vacuum. For several years prior, especially after oil prices skyrocketed in the early 1970s, Saddam did many good things for Iraq. He utilized Iraq's substantially greater oil proceeds that rose from half a billion dollars to tens of billions per year to build a national infrastructure of electricity to every village and town; schools, roads, modernization of the agricultural sector, and lifting the two-thirds of the poverty stricken population he found and reduced those poverty levels significantly. As a domineering, brutal dictator, he built a strong, loyal military to protect him from coups, especially from the predominant Shiite population.

He is also credited with establishing free universal compulsory education nationwide, which brought to hundreds of thousands of citizens the ability to read and write. He was also credited for granting free hospitalization to everyone, and gave subsidies to farmers. He created one of the most modernized public health systems in the Middle East, which won him an award from the U.N.'s UNESCO. He diversified Iraq's economy from singularly oil-based, promoting mining and developing other industries. But he also did many very bad things.

Politically, in a nation composed of three principal tribal loyalties, Shiia, the majority by far, Kurds, and Sunni, he brutally eliminated by execution all opposition in the Ba'ath Party. By using the nationalized banking system, he controlled lending to his loyalists, establishing a "cronyism" lending system.

As a result of the extraordinary expansion of Iraq's economy, more than two million people came to Iraq from other Arab countries, including hundreds of thousands of Palestinian technocrats and refugees, all of whom became loyal to Hussein who continued to strengthen his hold on the nation. As a result, Arafat supported Hussein during the first Gulf war.

It's interesting to note that the CIA colluded with Iran's Shah Mohamed Reza Pahlavi to finance and arm the Kurds of northern Iraq in opposition to Hussein's control. With the peace treaty between Iraq and Iran in 1975, that financing and arming of the Kurds by the CIA ceased. In the late 1980s, Hussein's military was accused by several international groups, including Amnesty International, of executing hundreds of thousands of Iraqis, including over 100,000 Kurds and Islamists in revenge for their efforts to overthrow him.

In the late 1970s, Iraq and Syria came close to unification. But if they had unified, Hussein would have been subordinate to Hafez Al Assad of Syria. As a result, Hussein cruelly set out to eliminate all opposition within the Ba'ath Party who were seeking unification with Syria, the same secular party of Assad.

When Sadat began negotiating unilaterally with Israel, Hussein broke all relations with Egypt.

* * * * *

When the Shah, strongman of Iran, was overthrown by the Islamic Revolution led by Rahallah Khomeini in 1979, the revolutionary Iranian Shiite Islamist forces grew menacingly, especially in Iran and Iraq, both countries with a large, majority Shiite population. Saddam Hussein believed the Islamists were a major threat to his secular government and that the extreme Islamists of Iran were influencing the majority of Shiites in Iraq. Earlier, Khomeini had been exiled from Iran by the Shah and temporarily located in Iraq. As he increased his Islamist influence, Saddam exiled Khomeini to France. From there, Khomeini was able to overthrow the Shah and return to Iran and assume the right of absolute power over Iran, after rescinding all his promises of women's rights, a secular state, freedom of the press, and free human rights.

Hussein sought to overthrow the Islamist regime of Iran that would, in his opinion, be in the best interests of the U.S. and the West.

In 1980, Iraq invaded Iran with the goal of occupying Khuzestan and declaring that province part of Iraq.

* * * * *

During the Iraq-Iran war, with the support from U.S., Western Europeans, and substantial financing from the fabulously rich Gulf oil-producing Arab states, Hussein became "The defender of the Arab World" against revolutionary Iran. Iraq became Iran's singular powerful enemy on its western border. Because of Hussein's "harsh treatment" of Iraq's communists, the Soviet Union refused to send aid to Iraq. Despite Iraq's violations of its borders with its neighbors and Hussein's cruelty, Iraq became known to many in the West as "an agent of the civilized world." The West conveniently ignored Hussein's use of chemical weapons against the Kurds and Iranians, and Iraq's efforts to develop nuclear weapons.

After the Egypt-Israel pact, the Israeli government felt more secure, especially from the south. But, as Saddam Hussein's Iraq grew stronger, Iraq became the new threat to the Israeli government.

The Israeli government came to see Iraq as their new major, powerful enemy, and Saddam Hussein as a major threat to its security, especially now that they had neutralized Egypt's leader and its' military. They felt something had to be done. With the influence of the pro-Israel "Neo-Cons" in Washington who believed likewise, they convinced newly elected President George W. Bush to change Washington's view of Hussein and invade Iraq to overthrow Saddam Hussein.

The stage was set. Extremist Arabs, angry over America's military presence in some Arab countries might turn on the United States.

When fourteen Al Qaida terrorists flew into New York's Twin Towers, interpreted as declaring war on the U.S., President George W. Bush, while initially sending forces to Al Qaida camps in Afghanistan to defeat that terrorist group, and the ultra-right extremist Taliban, he soon conjured excuses, many believed, in behalf of Israel, to invade and defeat Iraq and Hussein, declaring without convincing evidence that Iraq had enormous stocks of "Weapons of Mass Destruction" (WMDs), and was seeking to build atomic bombs, thus becoming a threat to Israel and U.S. interests. The plan of the U.S. Department of Defense Secretary Donald "Shock and Awe" Rumsfeld and his second, Paul Wolfowitz, meant to defeat Hussein, control Iraq, and install its own puppet Prime Minister, Mr. Chalabi, who agreed, once named as Prime Minister of Iraq, to sign a peace treaty with Israel despite being a fugitive in Jordan for crimes committed there. The invasion and overthrow of Hussein created a political vacuum, which appears at this date to be filling with Shiite Islamic extremists from Iran and a threat to Syria, Israel, and the United States. And today, after some many years of war, a trillion dollars spent, thousands of lives including thousands of young American men and women, Iraq is now "The Islamist Republic of Iraq," which is now controlled by extremist who have removed all equality, freedom of worship, freedom for women, and seek to accomplish the same in secular Syria as part of the so-called "Opposition ," which also includes Al Qaida, the Taliban, Jihadists, Islamists and extreme young Muslims bent on creating Islamist states across the entire Middle East.

Even then, after a trillion dollars and ill-advised post-invasion U.S. management, America left the war in Afghanistan, allowing the Taliban to resurge, and Al Qaida to resume its terrorist activities. U.S. troops were relocated from Afghanistan to Iraq. Thousands of America's finest lost their lives and thousands more returned impaired emotionally and physically damaged.

* * * * *

In November 2004, Yassir Arafat, still chairman of the Al Fatah, singular leader of the Palestine Liberation Organization, residing in Ramallah, a former totally Christian city, in the West Bank and still occupied and governed by Israeli forces, died. He was adored by most Palestinians for his leadership, seeking their national identity, esteem, and a homeland. He died due to causes still challenged by his heirs, family, and followers, many of whom remain suspicious of the true cause of his death.

The secret Oslo conference in 1993 convened by U.S. President William Clinton brought Chairman Arafat and then Prime Minister Yitzak Rabin of the moderate Labor Party of Israel together in an effort to seek resolution of the ongoing Israeli-Palestinian conflict. It was the first face to face agreement between the government of Israel and the PLO.

The secret conference, hosted by Norway's Fafo Institute, was completed on August 20, 1993. The conference in Oslo and was an outgrowth of what many considered a positive and constructive conference in Madrid in 1991.

The agreement was titled "Declaration of Principles on Interim Self-Government Arrangements," also called Declaration of Principles (DOP).

The Oslo Accords or DOP were adopted on August 20, 1993 and signed on the White House lawn on September 13, 1993 witnessed by Prime Minister Rabin, Chairman Arafat, and President Clinton and signed by Mahmoud Abbas for the PLO, by Shimon Perez, Foreign Minister of Israel, U.S. Secretary of State Christopher Wren, and Foreign Minister Andrei Kozyrev of Russia.

The Oslo Accord called for the creation of the Palestinian National Authority (PNA) to be responsible for the administration of the territory under its control. Still, in contradiction of the Oslo Accord, Israel continues to control much of the West Bank, and continues building new settlements to this day, in 2013, on taken land privately owned by Palestinians. Oslo also called for the withdrawal of the Israel Defense Forces (IDF) from parts of the West Bank that were not clearly defined, and Gaza. The Oslo Accord did not provide Palestinian statehood, but a five-year interim period during which the Palestinian Authority would control social issues including education, direct taxation, economic/financial issues and local police. After Rabin was assassinated, Benjamin Netanyahu became Prime Minister and great debate took place in Israel and Palestine and both sides provoked the other. Netanyahu declared the entire Jordan Valley would remain part of Israel for "security reasons." He rejected the Oslo Accords and encouraged more and more Jewish settlements in the West Bank.

Little was achieved save for the establishment of the

Palestinian Authority and its control over mostly social and internal issues. Still, Madrid and Oslo negotiations between the two parties can be considered positive steps in the continuum of negotiations between the two adversaries.

More peace conferences between the parties have taken place and even more have been sought. The U.S. has continued to seek peace at great cost between the parties with little success for too many decades.

But, peace and statehood for the Palestinians and Israel's quest for guaranteed security continues to elude the parties.

* * * * *

With regard to Gaza, Israel still controls its airspace, coastline, ports, industry, electric power and other infrastructure. In response, the Sunni, Islamist-oriented controlling regime of Gaza continues to be the most belligerent adversary of Israel, firing rockets into southern Israel, withstanding Israeli aerial attacks, and fighting the Palestine National Authority (PNA) whose President Abbas and cabinet continue to build and grow a viable economy in the West Bank and seeking Hamas' cooperation in obtaining peace with Israel. But Hamas does not appear to seek peace with Israel.

Peace may eventually come to the Middle East, but it is clear that can happen only when the human rights of the Palestinian people, who now are equal in population to the Jewish people west of the Jordan River, are restored. Only then can they self-govern their own

213

state without military or political occupation by any other country. And perhaps, somehow, restoring human rights to all in the Middle East, including those still controlled by family regimes as in Syria, albeit secular and relatively free and economically successful will have to occur in other states throughout the Middle East when Israel no longer attacked by anyone, Israel doesn't take more land from others and Israel agrees to a two state solution including a Palestinian state in the West Bank, dearly sought by the rest of the world return of the Golan, Gaza and East Jerusalem. And the people of Israel are convinced they are secure. Many wonder how this seeming conundrum will end. No one knows. But credit several U.S. presidents for continuing their tenacious efforts.

To this day, under the Likud Party government currently led by Prime Minister Benjamin Netanyahu, Israel continues to illegally, unilaterally take more and more private lands in the West Bank and East Jerusalem, and building more and more subsidized housing. In too short a time, the size of the West Bank remaining may be too small for a Palestinian state. But these two peoples disputing over a very small parcel of land someday must come to agreement, many believe, but only with the forceful leadership from the President of the United States. Until then, the world will continue to fret, wring hands, and watch as opportunity after opportunity withers, delaying decade after decade the incredible, positive potential of an enormously productive Middle East as a tourist mecca, high technology sector, trade, strong economies and hundreds of thousands of jobs.

Prosperity, stability and security for all the people of every nation.

Chapter 15
Camp David Accords Background

On November 9, 1977, Egyptian President Anwar Sadat, frustrated with the ongoing international conference seeking a regional peace in the Middle East being held in Geneva, shocked the world with a bold statement to his parliament of his plan to go to Jerusalem and speak to the Israeli Knesset. Ten days later, Sadat arrived in Jerusalem for a three-day visit that launched the first peace treaty between Israel and an Arab state.

Thus began unilateral peace negotiations between the two adversaries. Although Sadat addressed the Palestinian refugee problem and Israel's occupation of the West Bank and East Jerusalem taken by Israel during the Six- Day War in June 1967, he was not able to convince the Israelis to give back the West Bank and East Jerusalem.

Sadat's actions were totally inconsistent with the desires of the Arab world, which sought a regional solution including the return to the 1967 borders, including Syrian's Golan Heights, Gaza, the West Bank, East Jerusalem, and Egypt's Sinai Peninsula. It was also inconsistent with the desires of the U.S. and the rest of the world for a regional solution, including all Confrontation States.

To the Arab world, Sadat betrayed them, implicitly recognizing

215

the state of Israel, ignoring the plight of the Palestinians, and, as the U.S. also believed, was simply his effort to regain the Sinai of Egypt taken by Israel in 1967. He also felt it would solidify his political standing in Egypt and convince the West and NATO to help the ailing Egyptian economy.

Sadat did present to the Knesset his request for implementations of U.N. Resolutions 338 and 242 which required Israel to return all lands it captured during the Six-Day War in June 1967.

Israel, on the other hand, led by Menachem Begin and his hardline Likud Party, saw an opportunity for a bilateral peace agreement with the largest and most populace Arab country, separating Egypt from the rest of the Arab world and their efforts at an overall peace agreement. He also knew that without Egypt, the Arabs would be severely weakened as a military adversary.

Both Sadat and Begin sought to wreck the multi-national peace conference in Geneva, thwarting President Carter's efforts and the goals of his administration, of recognition of a Palestinian state and resolution of "the Palestinian issue" that would bring peace to the region. President Carter knew only a unilateral agreement would not by itself bring regional peace, but he believed that it could be the first step toward a regional peace agreement.

Sadat, whose nation had been a recipient of Soviet arms and aid during the Cold War, sought an alliance with the U.S. and not the Soviet Union. President Carter, although seeking a regional solution to the Middle East multi-national problems, brought Sadat and Begin with their teams to Camp David when it appeared negotiations would fail.

With Egypt's Sadat choosing to seek unilateral peace with Israel without apparent consultation with other Arab countries, it was analogous to Germany and Britain signing a peace agreement without including France, the U.S. and other countries of Europe conquered by the Germans. It simply was not acceptable.

Yet, President Carter of the U.S. inserted the U.S. into the negotiations in September.

To the Arab world, the U.S. was so biased in favor of Israel that, from their perspective, nothing good could come from these negotiations. As a result, the Arab world ceased communication with the U.S. They insisted they would not, could not, become part of those negotiations unless Israel was willing to return all lands captured in 1967, return human rights to the Palestinian people, and extend the right of return or recompense to the Palestinians for all lands taken. Of course, Israel refused to include any of those Arab demands, limiting any negotiations to only Egypt's Sinai.

As a consequence, Sadat became a pariah in the Arab world, and not one of the other twenty-one Arab countries offered any support or participation in the U.S. sponsored peace talks between Egypt and Israel.

At President Carter's invitation, the three heads of state met at Camp David for thirteen difficult days. Sadat and Begin hated each other. No trust, only antipathy stressed the negotiations. They would not speak with each other, so each had their own cabin. President Carter shuttled between their cabins seeking peace between the two and resolution of Palestinian human rights, removal of Israel's forces from the Sinai, West Bank, East Jerusalem, the Golan, and Gaza. Carter was reluctant to agree unless the Palestinian interests were included.

But Begin wanted only a bilateral agreement with Egypt (which meant only giving up the Sinai desert) and would not consider any resolution of Palestinian hopes for a state and self-determination. It served Israel's best interests, not for peace, but for economic and political reasons.

The talks were tenuous, stressful, and only through the tenacity, determination and unprecedented diplomatic effort by President Carter did the negotiations not fall apart. Carter continued to seek an agreement to include a homeland for the Palestinians. But Begin and his team would not relent. As a consequence, there were thirteen days of bitter polemics. As a compromise, two agreements became the Camp David Accords; first, a "Framework for Peace" in the Middle East and second, a Framework for the Conclusion of a Peace Treaty between Egypt and Israel. The second, leading to the Egypt-Israel Peace Treaty, was signed in March 1979. Both were accompanied by "side-letters" of understanding between Egypt and the U.S., and Israel and the U.S.

The first agreement had three parts: a framework for negotiations to establish an autonomous, self-governing Palestinian authority in the West Bank and Gaza, and to fully implement the U.N. Security Council Resolution 242. The Accords recognized the "legitimate rights of the Palestinian people," including removal of Israelis from the West Bank and Gaza. The Accords did not speak to Syria's Golan Heights, East Jerusalem, and Right of Return for Palestinians, or Lebanon.

The Accords were not the comprehensive peace that several U.S. Presidents had sought to achieve. The fate of East Jerusalem was deliberately excluded from the Agreements at Begin's insistence.

As for the Egypt-Israel Peace Treaty, within six months, Israel agreed to remove from Sinai its forces and 4500 Israeli civilian inhabitants in return for full diplomatic relations with Egypt and guarantees of free passage through the Suez Canal.

As a result, Begin got what he wanted and Sadat got the Sinai. But, Sadat would become a pariah for undermining the Geneva conference, and removing Egypt from the Arab bloc, removing Egypt's population and armed forces from the equation of "balance" the Arab countries sought.

In addition, the Accords included a commitment from the U.S. to annual subsidies to the governments of Israel ($3 billion, 5 million people), and to Egypt ($1.3. Billion, 50 million people), which continue to this day, some thirty-five years later. And U.S. humanitarian aid to Egypt, replacing the same Egypt had been receiving from the Soviet bloc.

While the Accords were considered a success in the United States, they were not consistent with earlier exploratory meetings with Sadat, Jordan's King Hussein, and Syria's Hafe

Al Assad (who met with President Carter in Geneva). Those meetings by Secretary of State Cyrus Vance and President Carter sought a regional peace agreement with Israel that included Israel's return of all occupied lands taken in 1967 including the Sinai, Syria's Golan, the West Bank, Gaza and East Jerusalem.

While the Camp David Accords brought peace between Israel and Egypt, they did not address the objectives of Washington and the entire Arab world.

Most Israelis supported the Camp David Accords. Israeli settlers in the Sinai, mostly right-wing extremists, demanded more Israeli settlers in the West Bank and Gaza as a quid pro quo for leaving the Sinai. They sought to prevent Israel's government from living up to its agreement.

Because the Accords did not include the participation of the U.N. General Assembly, the PLO and the U.N. Security Council, they were declared invalid in 1979. In Egypt, Sadat's unilateral peace efforts became universally hated by the Egyptian populace. Its economy remained a disaster, and bitterness against Sadat grew rapidly. Even Sadat's Prime Minister resigned from his office. Muslim fundamentalists became more vocal and more popular than ever. As a result of growing opposition, Sadat jailed more than 100 opposition politicians. To make matters worse, Israel bombed Iraq's nuclear facilities, annexed East Jerusalem and built heavily subsidized settlements in the West Bank.

Commerce between Egypt and its Arab neighbors collapsed.

Egypt suffered bread riots, Fundamentalists grew in favor, becoming a major threat to secular Egypt, portending a possible future Islamic State. Every Arab country severed diplomatic ties with Egypt, and very soon, ceased communication with the government of the U.S.

As a result of the Accords, Egypt was alone, Sadat a pariah, Islamist Brotherhood support grew rapidly, anti-American fervor throughout the Arab world grew rapidly, and America's Arab allies for decades turned their backs.

* * * * *

For eighteen months prior to the Camp David negotiations, while the Geneva Peace Conference was seeking an overall peace agreement with all Arab Confrontation States, European governments and America participating with the presence of the PLO, Egypt and Israel pursued secret talks in Morocco seeking a bilateral peace agreement, and dissolution of the Geneva peace conference. Even the U.S. government was kept in the dark as were the Arab League and the Arab countries. No one knew that the two countries were proceeding toward a bilateral agreement.

Even after the Camp David Accords were ceremoniously signed with a worldwide television audience, Washington did not know the positions of the Arab world which was deeply offended and angry.

King Hussein of Jordan, who had the most to lose, felt he had been personally insulted. Jordan had lost the West Bank and East Jerusalem in 1967 and had to accept hundreds of thousands of penniless Palestinian refugees, as did Syria and Lebanon. It was only after the Camp David Accords were signed did Washington begin to understand the depth of resentment the peoples and governments of the Arab world felt toward Sadat, Israel, and the U.S. Most, if not all the members of the Arab League, broke off diplomatic relations with Egypt and the U.S. As a result, the Carter Administration had no clue of the thinking of those governments, including the major producers of the world's crude oil.

After investing an incredible amount of political capital, time and energy into the Camp David negotiations, President Carter, Secretary of State Vance, and President Sadat convinced themselves that other Arab states would agree to join in the Accords. Secretary

Vance and President Carter had spent Carter's first year in office visiting the heads of states of several Arab states admirably seeking a means of restarting the multinational peace conference in Geneva, seeking a regional solution, but were faced with the secret ongoing unilateral negotiations between Egypt and Israel.

As a result, those leaders who Vance and Carter had consulted, Assad of Syria, King Khalid of Saudi Arabia, Hussein of Jordan, and President Sarkis of Lebanon, now felt they were betrayed in the U.S., Egypt, and Israel. As a result, they severed diplomatic relations with Egypt. Still, the U.S. erroneously believed "flying blind," with no communications, the other Arab states would join in.

From the "victory" signing of the Accords on September 17, 1978, the administration began to determine how best to learn the positions of the non-communicative governments of Saudi Arabia, Jordan, Qatar, Iraq, Bahrain, Syria, Lebanon, and the PLO, most of whom Carter hoped would ultimately join in the Camp David Accords and then, together with the U.S., rejuvenate a multilateral peace conference that would include solution to the "Palestinian problem," resulting in a return of all lands captured by Israel in 1967, and establishment of a Palestinian state in the West Bank.

Can there eventually be peace in the Middle East? The answer must be, "Yes" But it will likely be when both sides elect leaders of good faith in the God they profess to honor.

Camp David Accords

About the Author

As a first generation Syrian/Lebanese American, Sandy Simon aka Alexander Simon Eassa Chalhoub-Thomé-Zaine, has lived his life infused with a blending of the contrasting cultures of America and the Middle East. Mr. Simon is a graduate of the School of Architecture, Georgia Institute of Technology, and received his MBA from the Wharton Graduate School, University of Pennsylvania.

Since 1973, Mr. Simon has been active in Middle East affairs, its history, and current issues. For fourteen years he served as Senior Vice President of the National Association of Arab Americans (NAAA).

In 1978, Mr. Simon, together with three other officers of the NAAA, traveled to eight Arab countries at the request of Secretary of State Cyrus Vance on behalf of President Jimmy Carter seeking their private views of peace in the Middle East after the signing of the Egyptian-Israeli Camp David Accords, which did not include provision of a Palestinian State. As a result, the Arab world severed diplomatic relations with the United States and Egypt.

This book, Mr. Simon's seventh book and the fourth based on the Middle East, is a memoir of those meetings with Arab dignitaries based on verbatim notes and photographs taken on this fact finding mission.

Mr. Simon has walked the streets of Jerusalem, Beirut, Damascus, Amman, Tyre, and Sidon.

Camp David Accords